Close Reading Companion

McGraw Hill Education

Cover and Title Pages: Nathan Love

www.mheonline.com/readingwonders

Send all inquiries to:
McGraw-Hill Education
Two Penn Plaza
New York, NY 10121

ISBN: 978-0-02-132941-0
MHID: 0-02-132941-9

Printed in the United States of America.

5 6 7 8 9 RMN 20 19 18 17 16   B

Growing and Learning

STORYTIME

TRADITIONS

COMMUNITIES

INVENTIONS

TIME FOR KIDS

Figure It Out

One of a Kind

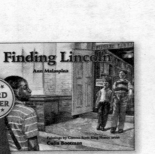

Meet the Challenge

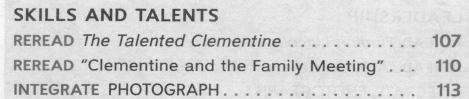

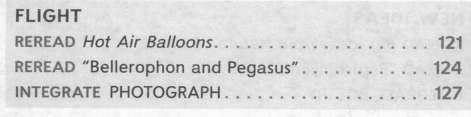

Take Action

(t)Liz Roll/FEMA Photo News; (b)©Ocean/Corbis

Think It Over

TREASURES

WEATHER

LEARNING TO SUCCEED

ANIMALS AND YOU

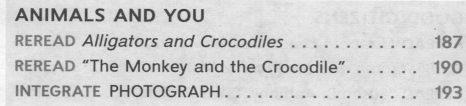

FUNNY TIMES

NASA/JPL-Caltech/N. Flagey (IAS/SSC & A. Noriega-Crespo (SSC/Caltech)

WOLF!

Literature Anthology: pages 10–31

? **How does the author show how the pig feels about the wolf?**

COLLABORATE

Talk About It Reread the last paragraph on page 17. Look at the illustration. Talk with a partner about how the pig feels.

Cite Text Evidence What clues help you see how the pig feels? Write text evidence in the chart.

Tip of the Week

Illustration	Text

Write The author shows how the pig feels about the wolf by _____

_____

_____

When I **reread**, I use illustrations to help me understand the characters.

Alicia

? How does the author help you understand how and why the wolf changes his mind?

COLLABORATE

Talk About It Reread page 18. Talk with a partner about what the wolf says to himself about the animals.

Cite Text Evidence What does the wolf think when he meets the pig, the cow, and the duck? Write text evidence in the chart.

QUICK TIP

I can use these sentence frames when we talk about what the wolf is thinking.

The wolf thinks to himself...

This helps me understand...

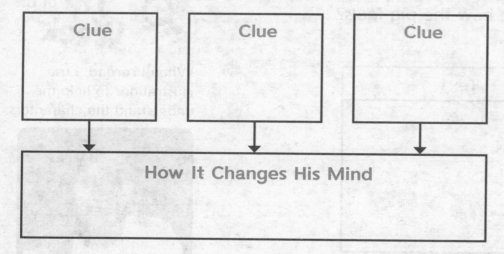

| Clue | Clue | Clue |

How It Changes His Mind

Write The author helps me see how the wolf changes by _____

_____

_____

? **How is the wolf different than he was when you first met him at the beginning of the story?**

COLLABORATE

Talk About It Reread page 24. Talk to a partner about how the wolf has changed.

Cite Text Evidence What words and phrases help you see what the wolf is like now? Use the chart to write text evidence.

Beginning	Page 24

Write I read that the wolf has changed because now _____

_____

QUICK TIP

I can compare the beginning and the middle of the story to understand the characters better.

Your Turn

How has learning to read changed the wolf's life? Use these sentence frames to focus your discussion.

At the beginning, the wolf...

I noticed that Becky Bloom...

That helps me see that the wolf...

Go Digital!
Write your response online.

Jennie and the Wolf

1   Jennie lived in a little cottage in the woods with her mother. They were very poor.

2   "Oh, dear, we have no more eggs! And it's almost time for dinner!" said Jennie's mother.

3   "I'll run to the market, mother!" said Jennie. "I'll take the shortcut!" She rushed out with her basket into the forest.

4   Deep in the forest, Jennie heard a loud moan. Walking on, she made a shocking discovery. A huge, gray wolf stood under a tree, crying!

5   "Please don't run away," the wolf said. "Could you help me? No one else will." The wolf held out his paw. A large, sharp thorn was stuck deep in his paw.

6   "Is this a trick?" Jennie asked. "I've heard stories about wolves eating people."

7   "Your knowledge of wolves is out of date," sighed the wolf. "Wolves don't eat people anymore. My brothers and I like to eat eggs. With ketchup!" The wolf cried and looked at his paw.

Reread and use the prompts to take notes in the text.

Underline two things that Jennie says that help you know what she's like. Write two words that describe her character.

1. _____

2. _____

Now circle two things the wolf says that helps you understand more about him.

COLLABORATE

Reread paragraph 7. Turn and talk with a partner about what the wolf said. Draw a box around words and phrases that show what the wolf is like.

8 Jennie was inspired to help. She knelt down and carefully removed the thorn. The wolf gently licked his paw. "Thank you. I will not forget your kindness!" the wolf promised. He bowed and disappeared into the forest.

9 Later, Jennie hurried home through the forest with her basket of eggs. "GRRRROOOOWLLLL!" A pack of hungry wolves appeared out of nowhere and blocked her path.

10 "What's in the basket?" snarled one wolf. "It looks like eggs!" cried another. "Where's the ketchup?" asked a third.

11 Then a voice roared, "Let her go!" The wolf whom Jennie had met earlier bounded down the path. "This girl helped me when no one else would." He told the pack how Jennie had helped him.

12 The other wolves moved aside. Jennie thanked her new friend, the wolf. Then she rushed down the path.

13 When Jennie got home, she helped her mother finish cooking. At dinner, she told the amazing tale of the gray wolf. Jennie also shared the moral she had learned:

14 *Help others and they will help you.*

Reread paragraph 8. Circle what the wolf says to Jennie.

COLLABORATE

Talk with a partner about how the illustration helps you understand how Jennie helps the wolf. Draw a box around the clues in the illustration that support your discussion.

Underline sentences that show how the wolf repays Jennie for her help.

? **How does the author use dialogue to help you understand more about Jennie and the wolf?**

COLLABORATE

Talk About It Reread paragraphs 7 and 8 on pages 4–5. Talk about why Jennie decides to help the wolf.

Cite Text Evidence What does the wolf say that helps you understand what the wolf and his brothers are like? Write text evidence in the chart and explain what it means.

What the Wolf Says	What It Means

Write The author uses dialogue to help me understand that _____

_____

_____

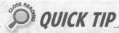
QUICK TIP

When I reread, I use what the characters say to help me understand why they do what they do.

? How do the poet and the authors of *Wolf!* And "Jennie and the Wolf" use words and phrases to show how characters can change?

COLLABORATE

Talk About It Read the poem. Talk with a partner about why Dragon-fly, Snail, and Mister Mouse go to the Flower of Mending.

Cite Text Evidence Underline words and phrases in the poem that tell what parts of each character need mending or fixing. Circle the stanza that tells where they go. Draw a box around what happens at the end of the poem.

Write The words and phrases used by the poet are like _____

_____

_____

_____

QUICK TIP

I can use the poet's words and phrases to help me understand how characters change. This will help me compare the poem to the stories I read this week.

The Flower of Mending

When Dragon-fly would fix
  his wings,
When Snail would patch
  his house,
When moths have marred
  the overcoat
Of tender Mister Mouse,
The pretty creatures go
  with haste
To the sunlit blue-grass
  hills
Where the Flower of
  Mending yields the wax
And webs to help their ills.

The hour the coats are
  waxed and webbed
They fall into a dream,
And when they wake
  the ragged robes
Are joined without a seam.

— Vachel Lindsay

Yoon and the Jade Bracelet

Literature Anthology: pages 34–51

? **How does the author help you understand how Yoon feels about the present her mother gives her?**

COLLABORATE

Talk About It Reread page 36. Turn and talk with a partner about what Yoon really wants for her birthday. How do you know?

Cite Text Evidence What words and phrases show how Yoon feels? Write text evidence here.

Text Evidence	How Yoon Feels

Write The author helps me understand how Yoon feels by _____

_____

Tip of the Week

CLOSE READING

When I **reread**, I can think about how the author uses words and phrases.
I look for text evidence to answer questions.

Walter

? **How do you know that jade is important to Yoon's culture?**

COLLABORATE

Talk About It Reread the last paragraph on page 39. Talk about what Yoon's mother says about jade.

Cite Text Evidence What clues help you see that jade is important in Yoon's culture? Write text evidence in the chart.

Jade Is Important	How Do I Know?

Write I know that jade is important to Yoon's culture because

_____

_____

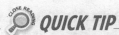 QUICK TIP

I can use these sentence frames when we talk about jade.

Yoon's mother uses words like...

This helps me understand that jade is...

? How does the author use what the children say to show that they are Yoon's friends?

COLLABORATE

Talk About It Reread page 47. Talk with a partner about what Yoon's classmates do and say.

Cite Text Evidence What do Yoon's classmates do and say when their teacher asks about the bracelet? Write clues in the chart.

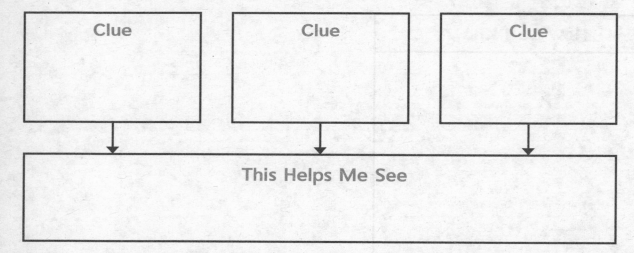

Clue	Clue	Clue

This Helps Me See

Write I know the children are Yoon's friends because the author

_____

_____

_____

QUICK TIP

I can use what the characters do and say to help me understand what is going on in the story.

Your Turn

How does Yoon change from the beginning of the story to the end? Use these sentence frames to organize your text evidence:

At the beginning, Yoon wants...

The author helps me see that...

At the end, Yoon...

Go Digital!
Write your response online.

Family Traditions

Celebrating a New Year

1   Chinese families celebrate Chinese New Year. Chinese New Year happens in January or February. It lasts about two weeks. The holiday means that winter is ending. Spring is on the way!

2   The traditions for Chinese New Year are very old. Adults give children bright red envelopes. Red stands for good luck and happiness. The envelopes are full of good luck money.

3   This holiday is also a time for feasts. Chinese families share sweet, smooth, rice cakes. Some families eat a whole cooked fish. They give oranges as presents. They eat noodles, too. These foods are symbols for a happy year and long life.

4   In most big cities families watch the Chinese New Year parade. Dragon dancers glide down the street. Lion dancers wear costumes in red, yellow, and green. Bands march by in rows. Their drums beat out happy tunes. People in traditional costumes go by on floats. They wave to the crowd. BANG! Watch out for firecrackers! They are part of the tradition, too. Loud sounds are symbols of a joyful time of year.

Reread and use the prompts to take notes in the text.

Reread paragraph 1. Put a star next to the sentence that tells what the Chinese New Year means. Write it here:

_____

_____

Now reread paragraphs 2–4. Underline Chinese New Year traditions.

COLLABORATE

Turn and talk with a partner about Chinese New Year traditions. Circle words the author uses to help you picture what some of the traditions are like.

Storytelling and Dance

[1]   Many Native American cultures have traditions of storytelling and dance. The stories are from long ago. Older people tell the stories to their children and grandchildren. They may use the culture's native language. The stories explain things in nature. They tell about the courage of early people.

[2]   Some Native American groups get together in the summer. They meet at big pow wows. These festivals celebrate culture through dance and music. Storytellers bring the old tales to life. The soft notes of a flute may help tell a story. The firm beat of a drum adds power. People from other cultures can watch and listen. Everyone enjoys the stories and learns about the traditions.

Reread paragraph 1. Circle two Native American traditions. Write them here:

1. _____
_____

2. _____

Underline what Native American stories explain and tell about.

COLLABORATE

With a partner, reread paragraph 2. Talk about how the author describes the festivals. Draw a box around the words and phrases she uses.

How does the author help you picture what traditions are like?

Talk About It Look back at your notes. Talk with a partner about how some families use traditions to celebrate.

Cite Text Evidence What words does the author use to help you picture what some traditions are like? Write them in the web.

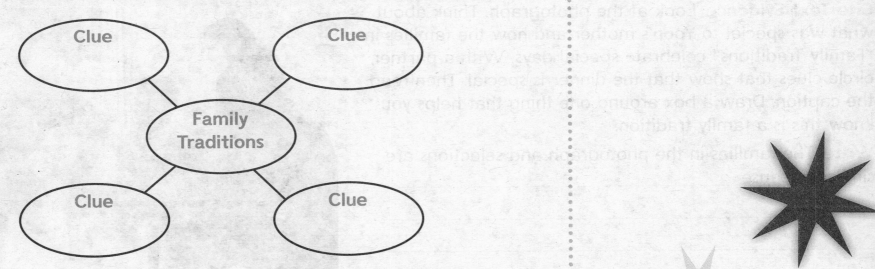

Clue

Clue

Family Traditions

Clue

Clue

Write The author helps me picture what traditions are like by

_____

_____

QUICK TIP

I can think about how the author describes traditions. This will help me complete my web.

? **How is the family in the photograph like the characters in *Yoon and the Jade Bracelet* and the people in "Family Traditions"?**

COLLABORATE

Talk About It With a partner, talk about what the family is doing in the photograph. Choose one clue that shows a tradition and talk about how you know it's important.

Cite Text Evidence Look at the photograph. Think about what was special to Yoon's mother and how the families in "Family Traditions" celebrate special days. With a partner, circle clues that show that the dinner is special. Then read the caption. Draw a box around one thing that helps you know this is a family tradition.

Write The families in the photograph and selections are similar because _____

_____

_____

_____

_____

Digital Vision/Alamy

This family lives in Richmond, Virginia. They celebrate every Thanksgiving at their grandmother's house.

Gary the Dreamer

? How is knowing what Gary did as a child important to understanding his autobiography?

Literature Anthology: pages 58–71

COLLABORATE

Talk About It Reread the first paragraph on page 61. Talk with a partner about how Gary played with his toys.

Cite Text Evidence What words and phrases help you picture how Gary plays with his toys? Write text evidence in the chart.

Text Evidence	What It Tells

Write I know Gary's childhood is important because it shows that

_____

_____

CLOSE READING

Tip of the Week

When I **reread**, I can use words and phrases to help me visualize. I look for text evidence to answer questions.

Gina

? **How does the author help you learn more about Gary's character?**

Talk About It Look at pages 62 and 63. Turn and talk with a partner about what you see and what it tells you about Gary.

Cite Text Evidence How is Gary different from his classmates? Write text evidence and explain how you know.

Gary	His Classmates	How I Know

Write The author helps me know more about Gary by _____

_____

_____

? **Why is _Gary the Dreamer_ a good title for this story?**

COLLABORATE

Talk About It Reread the last two paragraphs on page 69. Talk about how Gary uses the word _dreamed_.

Cite Text Evidence How does Gary use the word _dreamed_ to show how he has changed? Write text evidence in the diagram.

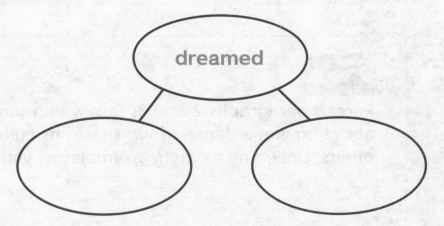

dreamed

Write _Gary the Dreamer_ is a good title for this story because it tells me that _____

_____

QUICK TIP

I can analyze how the author uses words to help me understand the story.

Your Turn

How does Gary Soto show how his dreams helped him become a writer? Use these sentence frames to organize your text evidence.

Gary describes his childhood by...

He shares his dreams to help me understand...

At the end, Gary writes...

Go Digital!
Write your response online.

Sharing Polkas and Pitas

Chicago, Illinois

[1]   Many people in Chicago come from Poland. Poland is a country in Europe. In a Polish community, you can see signs in Polish. You can smell Polish sausage. You can hear Polish music.

[2]   Dance and music are an important part of Polish culture. One dance group works hard to teach people about Polish culture. The performers in the Polonia Ensemble share their culture through music and dance. They wear colorful traditional costumes. They dance Polish dances, like the polka. They sing Polish songs. Polish dancers whirl in colorful costumes.

[3]   The group contributes to the community all year long. The dancers march in parades. They dance at festivals. Sometimes they travel to other cities and countries to share Polish traditions. They want to share their customs with everyone they meet.

Reread and use the prompts to take notes in the text.

Reread paragraph 1. Circle words that help you picture the signs of Polish culture in Chicago. Write them here:

1. _____

2. _____

3. _____

COLLABORATE

Reread paragraphs 2 and 3. Talk with a partner about how one dance group shares its culture with others. Underline as many examples as you can find.

Detroit, Michigan

[4] People from many Middle Eastern countries live near Detroit. The people of the community contribute in many ways. One important way is with food. The three Seblini brothers came from Lebanon. They wanted to share their culture with the community. How did they share? They opened a bakery!

[5] Every day, the brothers bake fresh pita and other Middle Eastern breads. They bake honey cake. They make spinach pie and stuffed grape leaves.

[6] The bakery is also a place to meet. People come from all over Detroit to enjoy food and friendship.

Look Again

[7] When you look at our flag, think about the 50 states. Then think about the different people and cultures within each state. Think about all the traditions people share.

Reread paragraph 4. What is one way people share their culture with their community? Underline text evidence.

Then reread paragraph 5. Mark the numbers 1, 2, 3, 4, and 5 beside the things that the brothers bake in their bakery.

COLLABORATE

Reread paragraph 6. Turn and talk with a partner about another way the brothers share their culture with the community. Circle the text evidence. Write the sentence here.

_____

_____

? How does the author use words and phrases to help you visualize how people share their cultures?

Talk About It Reread pages 18 and 19. Talk with a partner about how people in Chicago and Detroit share their cultures.

Cite Text Evidence What words and phrases help you picture how people share their cultures? Write three ways and how they help.

Text Evidence	What I Visualize

Write I can visualize how people share their cultures because

_____

_____

QUICK TIP

I can use my annotations to help me understand how people share their cultures with their communities.

? **How is the artist's purpose for creating this mural similar to why the authors of *Gary the Dreamer* and "Sharing Polkas and Pitas" share their stories?**

COLLABORATE

Talk About It With a partner, talk about the people you see in the mural. Look closely at what each worker does and how the artist shows how they each feel.

Cite Text Evidence Read the caption. Then circle three people in the mural. Write what they do in the margin next to them. In the caption, underline clues that help you figure out why the artist painted his mural.

Write The artist and authors share their art and stories to _____

_____

_____

_____

_____

QUICK TIP

I can find clues in the mural that show how the people in this community feel. This will help me compare text to art.

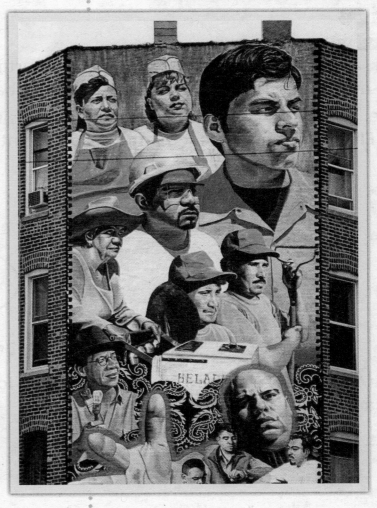

The artist painted this mural on a building in Chicago, Illinois. He used real people. It celebrates the community's hard-working Latin American people.

All Aboard!
Elijah McCoy's Steam Engine

Literature Anthology: pages 74-91

? How does the author help you understand how hard it was for Elijah's parents to send him to school in Scotland?

COLLABORATE

Talk About It Reread page 76. Turn to a partner and talk about how the author describes Elijah's family and their background.

Cite Text Evidence What words and phrases show how hard it was for Elijah's parents to send him to school? Write evidence in the web.

Elijah goes to school

CLOSE READING

Tip of the Week

When I **reread**, I can use what characters do to help understand more about them.

David

Write I know it was hard for Elijah's parents to send him to school because _____

_____

_____

? **How does the author hint that Elijah will work to change things for the grease monkey?**

COLLABORATE

Talk About It Reread page 82. Turn and talk with a partner about what a grease monkey does.

Cite Text Evidence What words and phrases show how Elijah feels about what a grease monkey does? Write text evidence in the chart.

Text Evidence	Elijah Thinks

Write The author helps me know that Elijah will change things by

_____

_____

? **How does the author use descriptive words to help you visualize what Elijah is doing?**

COLLABORATE

Talk About It Reread page 86. Talk with a partner about what Elijah thinks about as he invents.

Cite Text Evidence What words does the author use to help you understand how Elijah creates his invention? Write text evidence.

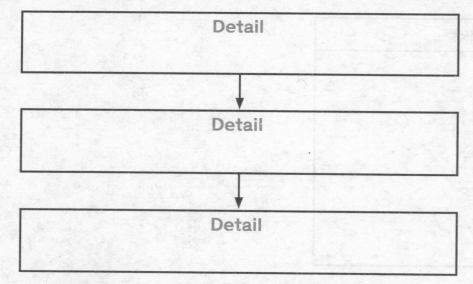

Detail

↓

Detail

↓

Detail

Write The author helps me visualize how Elijah invents by _____

_____

_____

QUICK TIP

I can use the author's words and phrases to visualize what Elijah is doing.

Your Turn

How does the author help you understand what it takes to invent something important? Use these sentence frames to organize your text evidence.

Monica Kulling writes about how Elijah...

She uses descriptive language to tell about...

This helps me understand that...

Go Digital!
Write your response online.

Lighting the World

A Bright Idea

[1]   In 1878, Thomas Alva Edison started an investigation. It would light up the world. Back then, homes and streets were lit by gas. People wanted to use electricity to light their homes. No one had found a good way to do it.

[2]   Edison and his helpers tried to make an electric light bulb. In an electric light bulb, a strip of material gets hot and glows. However, the strip burned up too quickly.

[3]   Edison examined many materials. None of them worked. He even tried beard hair. Then he tried bamboo. A strip of bamboo glowed for a long time inside the bulb. Edison's idea for the light bulb was a success.

[4]   Edison's solutions went beyond the light bulb. He designed power plants to make electricity. He designed a system to bring electricity into homes. Because of Edison, most people have light and electricity today.

Reread and use the prompts to take notes in the text.

Underline words and phrases in paragraph 1 that show that Thomas Edison was a successful inventor.

Reread paragraphs 2 and 3. Notice how the author uses sequence to explain how Thomas Edison and his helpers invented the light bulb. Number each step and write them here:

1. _____

2. _____

3. _____

COLLABORATE

Now reread paragraph 4. Talk with a partner about Edison's other solutions. Circle text evidence.

It's Electric!

[5]   Thomas Edison did many experiments with electricity. You can do an experiment with electricity, too. Investigate static electricity. Static electricity is an electric charge. It can build up when objects are rubbed together. Static electricity can pull objects together or push them apart.

Static Electricity Experiment

Materials
- scissors
- plastic comb
- wool scarf or sweater
- tissue paper

1. Cut several small pieces of tissue paper.
2. Place the pieces of paper on a table.
3. Hold the comb over the papers. What happens?
4. Now rub the comb on the wool about 10 times.
5. Hold the comb over the paper.

Reread paragraph 5. Underline how the author explains what static electricity is. Circle how static electricity builds up. Write what it is here:

_____

_____

COLLABORATE

Reread "Static Electricity Experiment." Draw a box around what you will need to complete this experiment. Talk with a partner about each step. Make a check next to the step that explains how static electricity builds up.

? **How does the author help you understand how inventors work?**

COLLABORATE

Talk About It Reread pages 25 and 26. Talk with a partner about the steps Thomas Edison took to invent the light bulb.

Cite Text Evidence How does the experiment help you understand how inventors work? Record your text evidence here.

Thomas Edison's Invention	Static Electricity Experiment

Write The author helps me understand how inventors work by

_____

_____

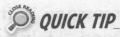
QUICK TIP

I can think about the steps in a process to help me understand what it takes to invent something.

? **How is the message in the song lyrics like the message in *All Aboard!* and "Lighting the World"?**

COLLABORATE

Talk About It Read the song lyrics. Talk with a partner about how the writers compare inventors and kids.

Cite Text Evidence Underline the question the writers ask. Then circle text evidence in the song lyrics that show how the writers answer it. Make a mark in the margin next to the lines that tell what the song's message is.

Write The message in the song is like _____

_____

_____

_____

_____

QUICK TIP

I use the words in the lyrics to understand the writers' message. This will help me compare the song to texts.

Inventive Minds

Inventions can change the world, you may say.

But did you know we're inventors today?

And now just like Orville and Wilbur Wright,

Our ideas are starting to take flight!

We all have inventive minds.

We're thinking of new ideas all the time.

Yes, kids have inventive minds.

We're using them ev'ry day of our lives!

Words and music by
Steve and Kathy Hoover

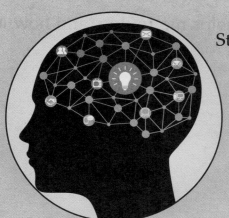

A Mountain of History

? How does the author show how Mount Rushmore can teach you about America's history?

Literature Anthology: pages 94–97

COLLABORATE

Talk About It Reread the first paragraph on page 95. Talk with a partner about why so many people visit Mount Rushmore each year.

Cite Text Evidence How does the author show that Mount Rushmore is an important national monument? Write clues here.

The author shows me that Mount Rushmore is important.

Write The author shows how Mount Rushmore teaches me about America's history by _____

_____

Tip of the Week

CLOSE READING

When I **reread**, I can think about how the author uses words and phrases. I look for text evidence to answer questions.

Patrick

©Hero/Corbis/Glow Images

? **How does the author help you understand Mount Rushmore's size and how big of a job it was to create?**

COLLABORATE

Talk About It Reread page 96. Turn and talk with a partner about why and how the monument was built.

Cite Text Evidence Why are "Carving a Monument" and "Think Big!" good headings for the sections? Write text evidence in the chart.

"Carving a Monument"	"Think Big!"	Author's Purpose

Write I understand how big Mount Rushmore is because the author

_____

_____

**QUICK TIP**

I can use these sentence frames when we talk about the author's purpose.

The author wrote about...

This helps me understand that...

Your Turn

Why is "A Mountain of History" a good title for this selection? Use these sentence frames to organize your text evidence.

The author says that Mount Rushmore...

That means the monument is...

This is a good title because...

Go Digital!
Write your response online.

A Landmark Street

1   Olvera Street is the birth place of Los Angeles. It started with a small group of settlers from Mexico. That was over two hundred years ago. Since then, Los Angeles has grown into a great city. And this city remembers its past. Olvera Street is part of the El Pueblo de Los Angeles Monument. This place keeps history alive.

2   Old buildings and museums on Olvera Street show visitors about its Mexican past. One of these is the Avila Adobe. It was built in 1818. It is the city's oldest building. It shows how people in California lived back then.

3   Families visit Olvera Street to learn about California history. They also enjoy the famous outdoor market. Musicians play cheerful Mexican and Spanish music. Folk dancers whirl in colorful costumes. Everybody has a good time on Olvera Street. And they learn about the past, too.

Reread and use the prompts to take notes in the text.

Reread paragraph 2. Circle facts the author includes that help you see how Olvera Street has a rich history. Write two facts on the lines.

1. _____

2. _____

COLLABORATE

Reread paragraph 3 with a partner. Place the numbers 1, 2, 3, and 4 beside the things people do when they visit Olvera Street. Talk about why Olvera Street is an important landmark.

? **How do you know that Olvera Street is an important landmark?**

COLLABORATE

Talk About It Reread the excerpt on page 31. Talk with a partner about what the author wants you to know.

Cite Text Evidence What words and phrases tell you that Olvera Street is important? Write text evidence in the chart.

 **QUICK TIP**

When I reread, I can think about the way the author organizes information.

Paragraph 1	Paragraph 2	Paragraph 3

Write I know that Olvera Street is an important landmark because the author _____

_____

? **How does F.F. Palmer show how the Sierra Nevada tells America's story like the national monuments and historical places in "A Mountain of History" and "A Landmark Street"?**

I see clues in the painting that help tell America's story. This will help me compare text to art.

COLLABORATE

Talk About It With a partner, talk about what you see in the painting. Choose some of the things you see and talk about how they help you learn about America's story.

Cite Text Evidence Think about why people would want to visit this place. Circle clues in the painting and the caption that show how the Sierra Nevada mountain range tells an important part of America's story.

Write F.F. Palmer's painting helps tell America's story like the stories I read this week because

_____

_____

_____

_____

_____

_____

Yale University Art Gallery

THE MOUNTAIN PASS.

British artist F. F. Palmer painted "The Mountain Pass" in 1867. This scene is in the Sierra Nevada, a mountain range known for its lakes, national parks, and monuments.

Roadrunner's Dance

? How does the author help you understand how the animals feel about Desert Woman?

Literature Anthology: pages 100–117

COLLABORATE

Talk About It Reread the first four paragraphs on page 106. Talk about why the animals went to talk to Desert Woman.

Cite Text Evidence What clues show how the animals feel about Desert Woman? Write text evidence and tell what they mean.

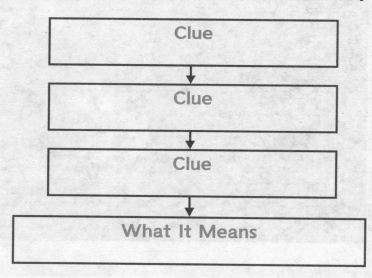

Clue

↓

Clue

↓

Clue

↓

What It Means

Write I know how the animals feel because the author _____

_____

_____

Tip of the Week

When I **reread**, I can use what the characters do to understand how they feel. I look for text evidence to answer questions.

Luis

? **Why does the author have each animal suggest a characteristic for the new animal?**

COLLABORATE

Talk About It Reread page 108. Turn and talk with a partner about what you notice about each animal's gift.

Cite Text Evidence How are the animals' gifts important to the new animal? Use text evidence to fill in the chart.

 **QUICK TIP**

I can use these sentence frames when we talk about each animal's gift.

Each animal gave a gift that...

The author chose to do this because...

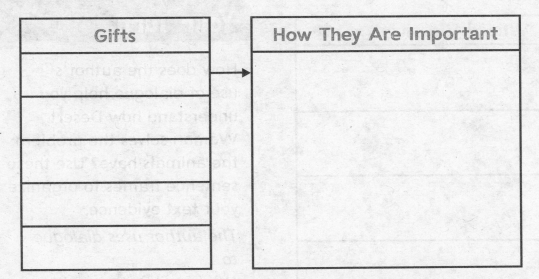

Gifts	How They Are Important

Write The author has each animal suggest a characteristic because

_____

_____

? **How does the author use descriptive language to help you visualize how Roadrunner improves?**

COLLABORATE

Talk About It Reread page 112. Talk with a partner about how Roadrunner practices running.

Cite Text Evidence What words and phrases help you understand what Roadrunner does to improve? Write text evidence in the chart.

Clues	→	What I Visualize
	→	
	→	
	→	
	→	

Write I can visualize how Roadrunner improves because the author

_____

_____

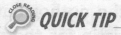
QUICK TIP
I can use the author's words to help me visualize what Roadrunner does.

Your Turn

How does the author's use of dialogue help you understand how Desert Woman solves the problem the animals have? Use these sentence frames to organize your text evidence.

The author uses dialogue to...

He describes the problem using...

This helps me understand how the animals...

Go Digital!
Write your response online.

Deltona Is Going Batty

Buzz! Buzz! Slap! Buzz! Buzz! Slap!

1   In Deltona, Florida, those are the sounds of summer. When summer comes, so do bugs.

2   The mayor of Deltona worked with a group of people to solve the bug problem. A man involved with the group came up with a fantastic answer. Bats! Bats like to eat bugs. Why not bring bats to Deltona? Let bats get rid of Deltona's bugs!

3   The mayor and the city government liked this idea. But people in Deltona had questions. Where would the bats live? Who would pay for bats?

4   The people who ran the city had to find answers. Then they had to decide what to do.

Reread and use the prompts to take notes in the text.

Reread the heading and paragraph 1. Circle a clue that tells you about the heading. Why is "Buzz! Buzz! Slap! Buzz! Buzz! Slap!" a good heading for this section? Write text evidence here.

_____

_____

COLLABORATE

Reread paragraphs 2–4. Underline words and phrases that the author uses to make this expository text interesting to read. Talk with a partner about the author's craft.

Write the numbers 1 to 5 beside the steps the city government took to solve their problem.

Local Government Decides

5   The mayor and other city officials met. They came up with a plan for the bats. It would not cost the town any money.

6   Bats can live in bat houses. Local business people will pay for them. Volunteers will put the bat houses in parks and public places.

7   The city officials talked to the people of Deltona about the plan. Their cooperation was important for the plan to work. Most people agreed. They wanted to try the plan.

8   The officials met again to vote on the plan. They decided to bring bats to Deltona!

Reread paragraphs 5 and 6. Underline the three-step plan the city officials came up with.

COLLABORATE

Reread paragraphs 7 and 8. Talk with a partner about how the author feels about Deltona's plan. Draw a box around the sentence that shows how the author feels.

Find Deltona on the map. Draw a circle around it. Talk about why the author includes a map.

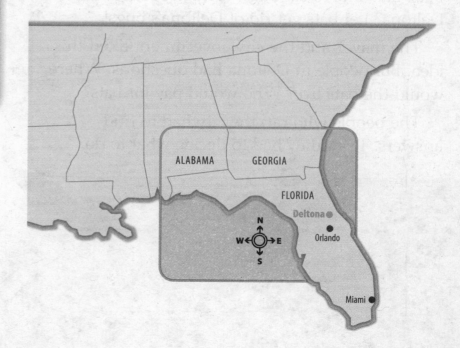

? **Why is "Deltona Is Going Batty" a good title for this selection?**

COLLABORATE

Talk About It Reread the excerpts on pages 37 and 38. Turn and talk with a partner about what Deltona's problem is.

Cite Text Evidence What do Deltona's city officials do about their problem? Use your notes to write text evidence in the chart.

Problem	Solution

Write "Deltona Is Going Batty" is a good title because _____

_____

_____

 **QUICK TIP**

When I reread, I can use text evidence to answer questions about author's purpose.

? **How does the photograph help you understand how people are solving a problem in the same way that the characters and community members do in *Roadrunner's Dance* and "Deltona Is Going Batty"?**

I see many people working together toward one goal. This will help me compare the photograph to text.

COLLABORATE

Talk About It Look at the photograph and read the caption. Talk with a partner about what the people are doing. Choose some people and discuss how they are working together to solve a problem.

Cite Text Evidence Underline text evidence in the caption that tells what the neighbors are doing. Circle five ways people are working together in the photograph.

Write The photograph, *Roadrunner's Dance*, and "Deltona Is Going Batty" help me understand that _____

_____

_____

_____

In this Amish community in Pennsylvania, people work together to build a new barn for one of their neighbors.

The Castle on Hester Street

How does the author use dialogue to help you get to know what Julie's grandparents are like?

Literature Anthology: pages 124–139

COLLABORATE

Talk About It Reread pages 128 and 129. Discuss with a partner how Julie's grandmother reacts to Sol's story.

Cite Text Evidence What clues in the dialogue help you get to know Julie's grandparents? Write text evidence in the diagram.

Tip of the Week

CLOSE READING

When I **reread**, I can use dialogue to learn more about the characters. I look for text evidence to answer questions.

What Do the Characters Say?

What Does It Mean?

Rachel

Write The author uses dialogue to _____

_____

_____

? How does the author show how Julie's grandmother and grandfather are different?

COLLABORATE

Talk About It Reread page 130. Talk with a partner about Julie's grandmother's version of their trip to America.

Cite Text Evidence Now reread the last paragraph on page 131. What clues help you see how different Julie's grandparents are?

Julie's Grandmother	Julie's Grandfather	How They Are Different

Write I know Julie's grandparents are different because the author

_____

_____

QUICK TIP

I can use these sentence frames when we talk about Julie's grandparents.

The author uses Julie's grandparents' stories to…

This helps me understand…

? **How do the illustrations help you understand how Julie's grandparents felt about living in America?**

COLLABORATE

Talk About It Look at the illustrations on pages 134 and 135. Turn to a partner and talk about what they show.

Cite Text Evidence What clues in the illustrations show how Julie's grandparents feel about living in America? Write clues in the chart.

How do Julie's grandparents feel?	
Clues on page 134	**Clues on page 135**
What They Mean	**What They Mean**

Write The illustrations help me understand _____

_____

_____

 **QUICK TIP**

I can use illustrations to look for more clues about how the characters feel.

Your Turn

How does Linda Heller use the stories Julie's grandparents tell to help you compare how they felt about coming to America? Use these sentence frames to help organize your text evidence.

Julie's grandfather's stories are...
Linda Heller tells her grandmother's point of view to show...
This helps me see that they...

Go Digital!
Write your response online.

Next Stop, America!

What Happened at Ellis Island

1   Immigrants crossed the ocean on crowded ships. When the ships arrived in New York harbor, smaller boats took them to Ellis Island. There the travelers hoped to become American citizens. Thousands of people came every day.

2   First, everyone had to have a check-up. The government didn't want sick people coming into the country. Some sick people stayed in the Ellis Island hospital until they were well. Someone with an eye infection was sent back across the ocean!

3   People also had to take a written test. They had to answer questions, give their names, and tell what country they were from. They had to tell where they planned to go. They had to promise to obey the laws of the United States.

4   After hours of waiting, most people got good news. The United States welcomed them to their new home.

Reread and use the prompts to take notes in the text.

In paragraph 1, underline how many people came to Ellis Island every day.

Reread paragraphs 2–4. Write numbers in the margin next to what immigrants had to do when they got to Ellis Island.

COLLABORATE

Reread paragraph 4. Talk with a partner about how immigrants felt about being allowed to stay in America. Draw a box around it the text evidence. Write it here:

_____

_____

Where They Went

5   From Ellis Island, the immigrants got on ferries to New York City. Many people's journeys ended there. Thousands settled near friends and family. They stayed in neighborhoods, such as Little Italy and the Bronx. Others had more traveling to do. They headed west or south, to other cities and states. Some went to places where they could get a job in a factory or a mine. Others found good farmland. No matter where the immigrants settled, they never forgot Ellis Island.

Reread the excerpt. Underline the sentence that helps you understand that most of the immigrants stayed in New York. Write it here:

_____

_____

Circle the places where they settled.

COLLABORATE

Talk with a partner about how Ellis Island was a memorable place for immigrants.

Draw a box around the text evidence to support your discussion.

? **How do the headings help you understand what it was like to immigrate to America?**

COLLABORATE

Talk About It Reread the excerpt on page 44. Talk with a partner about why "What Happened at Ellis Island" is a good heading.

Cite Text Evidence What clues in the headings and photographs help you understand the selection better? Write them in the chart.

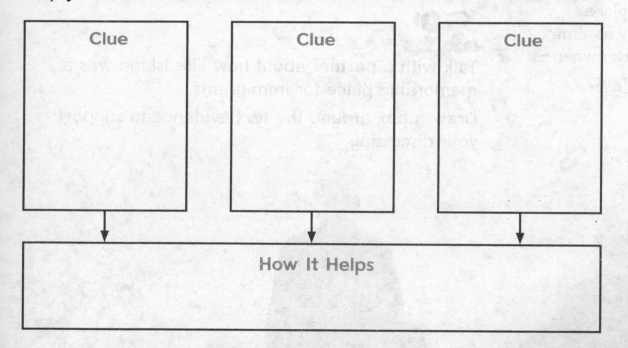

Clue	Clue	Clue

↓ ↓ ↓

How It Helps

Write The author uses headings to _____

_____

_____

? How do the photograph, *The Castle on Hester Street,* and "Next Stop, America!" help you understand why people came to America?

COLLABORATE

Talk About It Read the caption and look at the photograph. Talk with a partner about what you notice. Choose one person and describe what he is doing.

Cite Text Evidence What clues in the photograph help you understand what the boys are doing? Circle three different examples. Write words in the margin that tell what you see. Then underline words and phrases in the caption that give more information about what it was like to come to America.

Write The photograph, *The Castle on Hester Street,* and "Next Stop, America!" help me understand that people came to America to _____

_____

_____

_____

QUICK TIP

The photographer helps me understand how hard immigrants had to work. This helps me compare the texts with the photograph.

This photograph was taken in 1909 by photographer Lewis Wickes Hine. It is called "Immigrants in Night School" and shows a classroom in Boston, Massachusetts.

Vote!

? **How does the author help you understand that voting is important?**

COLLABORATE

Talk About It Reread page 150 and look at the illustrations. Talk with a partner about how important each person's vote is.

Cite Text Evidence What clues in the text and illustrations help you see that every vote counts? Write text evidence in the chart.

Text Evidence	Illustration Clues	How It Helps

Write The author helps me understand how voting is important by

_____

_____

_____

Literature Anthology:
pages 146–165

Tip of the Week

When I **reread**, I can use text evidence and clues from illustrations to help me understand more about the selection.

Marlon

? **How does the author use illustrations and speech bubbles to help you understand how people vote?**

COLLABORATE

Talk About It Analyze the illustrations and speech bubbles on pages 158–159. Talk with a partner about what it is like to vote.

Cite Text Evidence How do the pictures and words help you understand the voting process? Write text evidence in the chart.

How Illustrations Help	How Text Helps

Write Illustrations and speech bubbles help me understand _____

_____

_____

_____

QUICK TIP

I can use these sentence frames when we talk about how to vote.

The illustrations show…

The speech bubbles help me understand…

? **How does the author help you understand what happens at an election ceremony?**

COLLABORATE

Talk About It Reread pages 164–165. Look at the illustrations. Talk about what happens during and after an election ceremony.

Cite Text Evidence What clues show what happens during and after an election ceremony? Write text evidence here.

```
┌─────────────────────────────────────┐
│                                      │
│                                      │
└─────────────────────────────────────┘
                   │
                   ▼
┌─────────────────────────────────────┐
│                                      │
│                                      │
└─────────────────────────────────────┘
                   │
                   ▼
┌─────────────────────────────────────┐
│                                      │
│                                      │
└─────────────────────────────────────┘
```

Write The author helps me understand the election ceremony by
_____
_____
_____

QUICK TIP
When I reread, I can look for text evidence to answer questions.

Your Turn

How does the author help you understand how American citizens are responsible for the way our government works? Use these sentence frames to help organize your text evidence.

Eileen Christelow organizes the text by...

She includes many examples of...

That helps me understand...

Go Digital!
Write your response online.

A Plan for the People

A Summer of Arguments

1 The meetings began on a hot day in May 1787. The delegates gathered together in the Philadelphia State House. They closed the windows because the meetings were secret. It was hot in the State House. When they opened the windows to cool off, bugs flew in. The delegates argued all summer in the hot, buggy rooms. Making a new plan for government was not easy or fun.

2 Some delegates wanted one person to run the new government. Others thought a group should be in charge. They all agreed on one thing. A group should make laws for the country. But they disagreed on how to pick these leaders. The famous inventor and statesman Benjamin Franklin attended the meetings. He wondered how the groups could ever make any decisions.

Reread and use the prompts to take notes in the text.

Reread paragraph 1. Underline words that help you visualize what the Philadelphia State House was like during the meetings.

COLLABORATE

Talk with a partner about what the delegates agreed and disagreed about in paragraph 2. Circle the things they disagreed about.

Why is "A Summer of Arguments" a good heading for this section? Use your annotations to explain.

_____

_____

_____

Making a Plan

[3]   The delegates wrote their plan and called it the United States Constitution. The Constitution was only a few pages long, but it was full of big ideas. The Constitution shows how our government works. It says that people are in charge of the government. People vote to pick their leaders. These leaders run the government for the people.

A Government That's Fair to All

[4]   The delegates planning the Constitution met for four months. They thought the Constitution was a good plan. But not all delegates signed it on September 15, 1787. Some of them wanted to make sure the government protected people's rights, too. A right is something you are allowed to have or do. In 1791, Congress changed the Constitution to protect the rights of American citizens. One right allows people to speak freely. These changes were called the Bill of Rights.

Underline the sentences in paragraph 3 that help you understand more about the Constitution.

COLLABORATE

Reread paragraph 4. Talk with a partner about how the author uses cause and effect to explain how the Bill of Rights was created.

Circle what happened when some delegates decided not to sign the Constitution.

What was the effect? Circle it and write it here.

_____

_____

_____

? How does the author use headings to help you understand how America's leaders wrote the Constitution?

COLLABORATE

Talk About It Reread the headings on pages 51–52. Talk with a partner about why the author uses the headings to organize the text.

Cite Text Evidence How do the headings help organize and explain the topic? Write text evidence in the web.

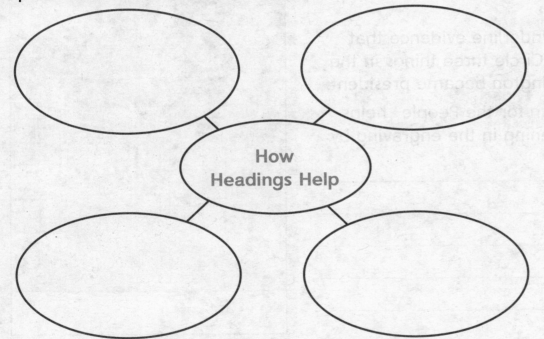

How
Headings Help

Write The author uses headings to help me understand _____

_____

_____

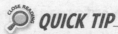
QUICK TIP
When I reread, I use headings to help me understand details about the topic.

? How does the information you read in *Vote!* and "A Plan for the People" help you understand what is happening in the engraving?

COLLABORATE

Talk About It With a partner, discuss what you see in the engraving. Read the caption and talk about how the authors of the selections and the artist who created the engraving show how people make government work.

Cite Text Evidence Reread the caption. Underline evidence that tells how people make government work. Circle three things in the photograph that show how George Washington became president.

Write The information in *Vote!* and "A Plan for the People" helps me understand more about what is happening in the engraving by

_____

_____

_____

_____

_____

_____

QUICK TIP

I see George Washington in the middle of the engraving. This helps me compare text to art.

WASHINGTON TAKING THE OATH AS PRESIDENT,
APRIL 30, 1789, ON THE SITE OF THE PRESENT TREASURY BUILDING, WALL STREET, NEW YORK CITY.

This engraving shows George Washington taking the oath of office on April 30, 1789. Americans voted for Washington and on this day, he was sworn in as their President.

Whooping Cranes in Danger

Literature Anthology:
pages 172–183

? How does the author organize the text so that you want to read more about puppet parents?

COLLABORATE

Talk About It Reread the last paragraph on page 175. Talk with a partner about what makes you want to read more about cranes.

Cite Text Evidence What does the author do to create more interest in puppet parents? Record text evidence in the chart.

What the Author Does	What I Want to Do
	→
	→

Write The author organizes the text by_____

_____

CLOSE READING

Tip of the Week

When I **reread**, I can find text evidence and think about how the author organizes information to make the selection more interesting to read.

Rhett

Why is "The Biggest Parent of Them All" a good heading for the section that describes the plane?

Talk About It Reread page 177. Talk with a partner about what the section is about.

Cite Text Evidence What clues show why the author chose the heading "The Biggest Parent of Them All"? Write them in the web.

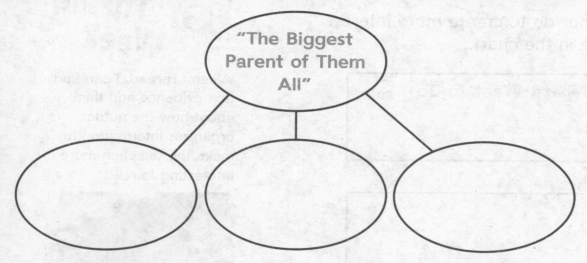

"The Biggest Parent of Them All"

Write "The Biggest Parent of Them All" is a good heading because

_____

_____

_____

QUICK TIP

I can use these sentence frames when we talk about why the author chose the heading.

I read in this section that…

This helps me see that "The Biggest Parent of Them All" is…

? **What does the author want you to know by using the word** *beginning* **at the end of the selection?**

COLLABORATE

Talk About It Reread "A New Beginning" on page 183. Talk with a partner about what will happen next to the whooping cranes.

Cite Text Evidence What clues help you understand the whooping cranes' new beginning? Write text evidence in the chart.

Text Evidence	"A New Beginning"

Write The author uses *beginning* at the end of the selection to

_____

_____

_____

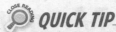
QUICK TIP
When I reread, I can think about the author's words and phrases to understand more about the whooping cranes.

Your Turn

How does the author show that saving the whooping cranes is important? Use these sentence frames to organize your text evidence

The author thinks the scientists are...

She shows that the survival of the whooping crane is important by...

I know that she thinks that...

Go Digital!
Write your response online.

Help the Manatees!

Why Are Manatees in Trouble?

[1]   People in Florida are worried. The manatees are in trouble. Hundreds of these super-sized marine mammals are dying every year. The population dropped from 3,000 to 2,500 in just twelve months. What caused the problem? People.

[2]   Manatees make their home in warm, shallow water. They live in Florida rivers and bays and in the ocean. They eat weeds and grasses that grow in water.

[3]   Manatees don't have many enemies because they are so large. After all, they're related to elephants! However, people have threatened their habitat. Many people live in Florida now. Lots of people take vacations there, too. More people than ever are using the manatees' habitat.

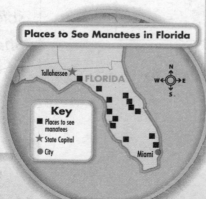

Places to See Manatees in Florida

Tallahassee ★   FLORIDA

Miami

Key
■ Places to see manatees
★ State Capital
● City

Reread and use the prompts to take notes in the text.

Circle clues in paragraph 1 that tell why people are worried about manatees. Write the reason here:

_____

_____

_____

Underline the sentence in paragraph 3 that helps you understand how big manatees are. Write it here:

_____

COLLABORATE

Talk with a partner about what people are doing that threatens the manatee. How does the map help you understand that better? Circle clues in the map.

Manatees can be seen throughout Florida. They live along the coast, and in rivers, springs, and bays.

Taking Action

1. The Save the Manatee Club has taken action to help manatees. The group educates people about these gentle giants. They teach kids and grown-ups how to keep the manatees safe and healthy. They rescue injured manatees. They work to change laws to help manatees.

2. The club gives away banners and signs. These remind boaters to go slow around manatees. The group also teaches people to use less water. Manatees need resources such as clean water.

3. Now people in Florida are more careful when they use the manatees' habitat. Manatees have a better chance to survive. They can thank their friends in the Save the Manatee Club!

Reread paragraphs 1 and 2. Underline the ways the Save the Manatee Club is working to help manatees.

COLLABORATE

Reread paragraph 3. Talk with a partner about how you know the club is successful. Circle the text evidence and write it here:

_____

_____

Draw a box around the sentence that goes with the photograph.

Slow Please

Manatees Below

? How does the author use text features to help you understand that people need to protect the manatees?

COLLABORATE

Talk About It Look at the text features on pages 58 and 59. Talk with a partner about what they help you understand.

Cite Text Evidence What clues help you understand why the author uses text features? Write the evidence here.

Map	Photograph	How They Help

Write The author uses text features to help me understand _____

_____

QUICK TIP

When I reread, I use text features to help me understand more about the topic.

COLLABORATE

? How is the photographer's message similar to what the authors want you to know in *Whooping Cranes in Danger* and "Help the Manatees!"?

QUICK TIP

In the photograph, I see a volunteer helping a dog. This will help me compare the photograph to text.

Talk About It Look at the photograph and read the caption. Talk with a partner about how the volunteer is helping Miss Daisy.

Cite Text Evidence What clues in the photograph show the volunteer doing the same type of things that the people in the selections did? Circle them. Then reread the caption and underline text evidence that explains why the volunteer is helping the dog.

Write I understand the message in the photograph and selections because the photographer and authors _____

_____

_____

_____

After Hurricane Katrina, this volunteer helped to take care of animals who lost their homes. The hurricane destroyed many homes in Louisiana. Here, Miss Daisy, a miniature poodle, gets cleaned up on Sept. 8, 2005.

The Inventor Thinks Up Helicopters

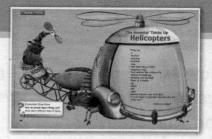

Literature Anthology:
pages 188–190

? How does the poet's use of alliteration help you visualize a helicopter?

COLLABORATE

Talk About It Reread page 189. Talk with a partner about how the poet's word choice affects the feel of the poem.

Cite Text Evidence How does alliteration help you picture a helicopter? Write text evidence in the chart.

Alliteration	I Visualize

Write The poet's use of alliteration helps me _____

_____

Tip of the **Week**

When I **reread**, I can find examples of figurative language. It helps me visualize the poems.

Sophia

Ornithopter

? How does the poet use descriptive language to help you understand the flight of the ornithopter?

COLLABORATE

Talk About It Reread page 190. Talk with a partner about how the poet describes how the ornithopter flies.

Cite Text Evidence What words and phrases describe the flight? Write text evidence in the word web.

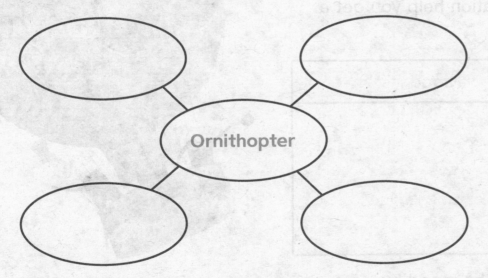

Ornithopter

Write I understand how an ornithopter flies because the poet

_____

_____

Your Turn

Think about the two poems you just read. How do the poets help you understand how people invent things? Use these sentence frames to organize your text evidence.

The inventors' machines…

The poet of "The Inventor Thinks Up Helicopters"…

The poet of "Ornithopter"…

Go Digital!
Write your response online.

Montgolfier Brothers' Hot Air Balloon

? How does the poet use the illustration to set the mood for the poem?

COLLABORATE

Talk About It Look at the illustration on page 192. Talk with a partner about what mood the illustration sets for the poem.

Cite Text Evidence What clues in the illustration help you get a feel for the poem? Write them in the chart.

Clues	Mood

Write The author uses the illustration to set the mood by _____

_____

_____

CLOSE READING 🔍 **QUICK TIP**

When I reread, I notice how the author uses illustrations to set the mood for the poem.

? How does the author's use of rhyme help you visualize the details of the hot air balloon's flight?

COLLABORATE

Talk About It Reread the poem on page 193. Talk with a partner about the words that rhyme and how they help you picture the flight.

Cite Text Evidence What rhyming words help you visualize the hot air balloon's flight? Find text evidence and write what you picture.

Montgolfier Brothers' Hot Air Balloon

Words	→	I Visualize
	→	
	→	

Write The author uses rhyme to help me visualize _____

_____

 **QUICK TIP**

I can use these sentence frames when we talk about rhymes:

The rhymes in the poem help me...

They help me visualize...

? How does Helen Leah Reed and the poets who wrote the poems you read this week help you understand how people figure things out?

COLLABORATE

Talk About It Read "A Curiosity." Talk with a partner about how the boy figures things out.

Cite Text Evidence Circle words and phrases in the poem that show the boy is curious. Choose a poem you read this week and think about how the poet describes how people invent things.

Write Helen Leah Read and the poets help me understand how people figure things out by _____

_____

_____

_____

QUICK TIP

I can use the poet's words and phrases to help me understand the boy in the poem. This will help me to compare it to the other poems I read this week.

"A Curiosity"

I knew a little boy, not very long ago,
Who was as bright and happy
    as any boy you know.

He had an only fault,
    and you will all agree
That from a fault like this a boy
    himself might free.

"I wonder who is there, oh, see!
    now, why is this?"

And "Oh, where are they going?"
    and "Tell me what it is?"

Ah! "which" and "why"
    and "who," and "what"
    and "where" and "when,"

We often wished that
    never need we
    hear those words again.

— Helen Leah Reed

Martina the Beautiful Cockroach

? How does the author help you visualize how Martina feels about Don Cerdo, the pig?

Literature Anthology: pp. 194–213

COLLABORATE

Talk About It Reread page 205. Talk with a partner about how Don Cerdo smells to Martina and what she does.

Cite Text Evidence What clues help you understand how quickly Martina wants to get rid of Don Cerdo? Write evidence and explain why it's important.

Tip of the Week

When I **reread**, I can use the author's words and phrases to help me understand how a character feels. I use text evidence to support my answers.

Don Cerdo	What Martina Does	I Visualize

Write The author helps me visualize how Martina feels about Don Cerdo by _____

_____

Nya

? **How do you know what kind of character Don Lagarto is?**

COLLABORATE

Talk About It Reread page 207. Talk with a partner about how the author describes Don Lagarto, the lizard.

Cite Text Evidence What clues helps you get to know what the lizard is like? Write text evidence in the chart.

Clues	What It Means

Write I know what kind of character Don Lagarto is because the author _____

_____

QUICK TIP

I can use these sentence frames when we talk about the lizard.

The author describes the lizard...

I know he is...

? **How does the author help you understand how the little mouse and Martina are perfect for each other?**

QUICK TIP

When I reread, I can compare characters to help me understand why they do what they do.

COLLABORATE

Talk About It Reread pages 212 and 213. With a partner talk about how the little mouse and Martina are alike and different.

Cite Text Evidence What details help you compare the little mouse and Martina? Write text evidence in the chart.

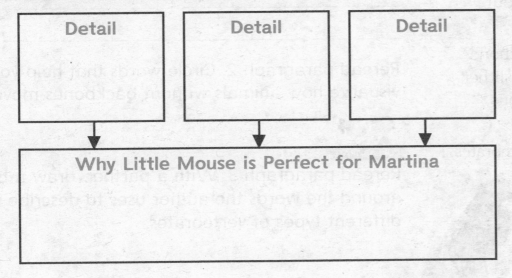

Detail	Detail	Detail

Why Little Mouse is Perfect for Martina

Write The author helps me understand that the little mouse is perfect for Martina by _____

_____

Your Turn

How does Carmen Agra Deedy help you predict how the coffee test will turn out for each character? Use these sentence frames to organize your text evidence.

Carmen Agra Deedy describes each animal by...

Then she...

This helps me understand why Martina...

Go Digital!
Write your response online.

Get a Backbone!

1   Most animals in the world fit in one of two groups. Some have backbones. The others do not. People, lizards, owls, frogs, and sharks all have backbones. Touch the back of your neck. That's where your backbone starts. It's a string of bones that goes all the way down your back to your tailbone.

2   What would you be like without a backbone? You couldn't walk or sit up. You'd have to slither around like a worm or swim like an octopus. Those animals have no backbones.

3   Animals with backbones are called vertebrates. All vertebrates have backbones. However, not all vertebrates are alike. They have different features. Some are tiny. Others are huge. Some swim, while others fly.

4   Vertebrates can be birds, amphibians, fish, reptiles, or mammals. Animals in each group share a unique quality that

Reread and use the prompts to take notes in the text.

Underline how the author helps you understand what a backbone is in paragraph 1. Look at the photograph and label. How does it help you understand more about what a backbone looks like? Use text evidence to write your answer:

_____

_____

Reread paragraph 2. Circle words that help you visualize how animals without backbones move.

COLLABORATE

Reread paragraph 3. With a partner, draw a box around the words the author uses to describe the different types of vertebrates.

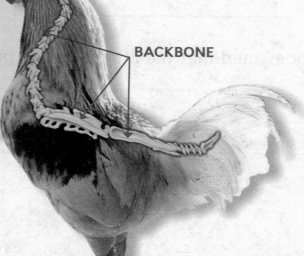

BACKBONE

Birds

5   Most birds can fly, but bees and bats can, too! Some birds, like ostriches and penguins, can't fly at all. Ostriches run. Penguins walk and swim. So what makes birds special?

6   Feathers, of course! Feathers keep birds warm. They can help birds to fly and steer through the air. The color of a bird's feathers can help it hide from predators or attract other birds.

Reptiles

7   Lizards and snakes are reptiles. All reptiles have scales covering their bodies.

8   Because reptiles are cold-blooded, they must live in warm places. Some snakes, turtles, and crocodiles live mostly in warm water. Some reptiles live in dry deserts. Most reptiles have low bodies, four short legs, and a tail. Only snakes have no legs at all.

Reread paragraphs 5 and 6. Number in the margins the ways that birds can be different from each other. Then, underline the sentence that states what all birds have in common.

COLLABORATE

Reread paragraph 8. Talk with a partner about what the word *cold-blooded* means. Circle how the author helps you understand what that means.

Then, draw a box around the places that reptiles live. Write them here:

1. _____

2. _____

? How does the author organize the information to help you understand more about backbones?

COLLABORATE

Talk About It Reread the excerpt on page 70. Talk with a partner about what the author does to make the information easier to understand.

Cite Text Evidence How does the author organize the information? Write evidence in the chart.

Text Evidence	How It Helps

Write The author helps me understand about backbones by _____

_____

_____

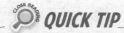

CLOSE READING **QUICK TIP**

When I reread, I can use the way the author organizes information to understand the topic better.

Integrate

? How is the way the artist shows the unique traits of the zebra in his painting similar to the way the authors highlight animal features in *Martina the Beautiful Cockroach* and "Get a Backbone!"?

COLLABORATE

Talk About It Look at the painting and read about it in the caption. Talk with a partner about what makes this animal unique.

Cite Text Evidence Underline text evidence in the caption that tells how the zebra is unique. Then circle two clues in the painting that show how the artist used his craft to show you. Think about how the authors of *Martina the Beautiful Cockroach* and "Get a Backbone!" used words and phrases to do the same.

Write Both the artist and the authors show unique animal traits by_____

_____

_____

_____

_____

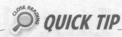 **QUICK TIP**

I can use details in the painting to help me compare it to what I read this week.

George Stubbs, an English artist, painted this oil painting in 1763. It is the first zebra to be seen in England. In "Zebra," George made sure his painting looked exactly like the live animal. He painted the zebra's ears facing in the backward direction and made sure the stripes were the same.

Finding Lincoln

? How does the author help you visualize how Louis feels about the library?

Literature Anthology:
pages 220–235

COLLABORATE

Talk About It Reread page 226. Talk with a partner about what Louis thought before he went into the library and how he felt when he got inside.

Cite Text Evidence What clues help you understand how Louis feels at the library? Use the chart to write evidence to support your answer.

Tip of the Week

CLOSE READING

When I **reread**, I can use how the author describes what the character is thinking to help me understand more about him. I use text evidence to answer questions.

Text Clues	How Louis Feels	How I Know

Write The author helps me visualize how Louis feels about the library by _____

_____

Isabella

? **How do you know that the librarian is nervous about helping Louis?**

QUICK TIP

I can use these sentence frames when we talk about how the librarian feels.

The author tells me that the librarian...

This helps me understand...

COLLABORATE

Talk About It Reread the fourth paragraph on page 229. Talk with a partner about the risk the librarian is taking.

Cite Text Evidence What clues tell you that the librarian is nervous about helping Louis? Write text evidence in the chart.

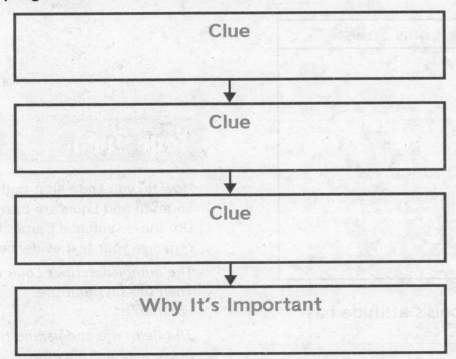

Clue

↓

Clue

↓

Clue

↓

Why It's Important

Write I know that the librarian is nervous about helping Louis because the author _____

_____

? **How does the author help you understand how Louis's attitude toward going to the library has changed?**

COLLABORATE

Talk About It Reread page 235. Talk about what Louis is thinking before he falls asleep.

Cite Text Evidence What clues tell about how Louis feels about the library? Write text evidence in the chart.

Clues	How Louis Feels

Write The author helps me understand how Louis's attitude has changed about the library by _____

_____

_____

QUICK TIP

When I reread, I can use what the characters are thinking to help me understand how they have changed.

Your Turn

How do you know that both the librarian and Louis are brave? Use these sentence frames to organize your text evidence.

The author describes Louis by...
Then she says that the librarian is...

This helps me understand how brave they are because...

Go Digital!
Write your response online.

A Great American Teacher

Everyone Gets a Chance

1 In 1904, many African Americans moved to Daytona Beach, Florida to build a railroad. Mary decided to open a school for the railroad workers' children.

2 Building a school was hard work. Mary rented an old cottage for the school. Her neighbors helped her fix it up. The first students were five girls and Mary's own son. The students used burnt wood for pencils and crushed berries for ink. Mary biked around town asking people to contribute to the school. More students came. They sold vegetables and gave concerts to raise money for the school.

Mary McLeod Bethune

Reread and use the prompts to take notes in the text.

Underline the sentence in paragraph 1 that shows the reason why Mary opens a school.

Reread paragraph 2. Number the steps that show what Mary did to open her school. Circle the clues that tell how they raised money. Write them here:

1. _____

_____

2. _____

_____

COLLABORATE

Talk with a partner about how Mary's hard work contributed to the school's success.

Changing Lives

3 By the 1920s, Mary needed a bigger building for her school. She opened a larger school that joined with another school nearby. The school became Bethune-Cookman College.

4 Mary grew up poor, but she helped many African Americans have more opportunities. Because of her, many African Americans received an education. She was a leader who was inspired to teach. Mary's story still inspires us.

Mary with her students in 1905

Reread paragraph 3. Underline the clue that helps you know that Mary's school was successful. Write it here:

_____

_____

How do you know why Mary's school became the Bethune-Cookman College? Make a mark in the margin beside the clue that explains it.

COLLABORATE

Reread the last paragraph. Talk with a partner about why the author chose to use the word *inspire*. Circle where it is used.

? **How does the author help you understand how hard Mary McLeod Bethune worked?**

COLLABORATE

Talk About It Reread paragraph 2 on page 77. Turn and talk to a partner about everything Mary did to build her school.

Cite Text Evidence What details does the author include that show Mary was a hard worker? Write text evidence in the web.

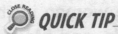
QUICK TIP
When I reread, I can look for details about what the character does.

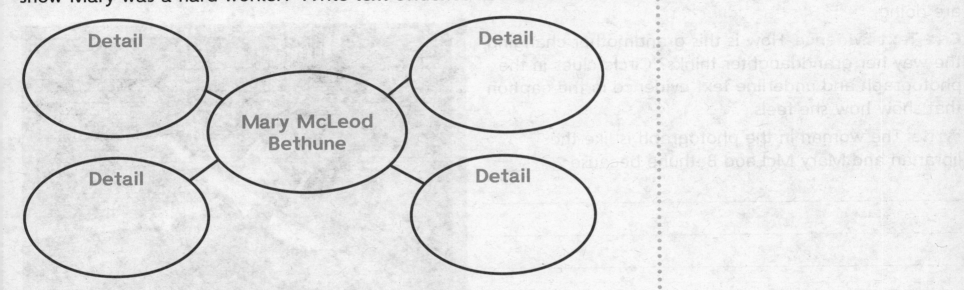

```
  Detail                    Detail


            Mary McLeod
              Bethune

  Detail                    Detail
```

Write I know that Mary was a hard worker because the author

_____

_____

_____

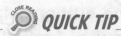

? How does the woman in the photograph, the librarian in *Finding Lincoln,* and Mary McLeod Bethune in "A Great American Teacher" help you understand how one person can change the way you think?

COLLABORATE

Talk About It Read the caption and look at the photograph. Talk with a partner about what the grandmother and her granddaughter are doing.

Cite Text Evidence How is this grandmother changing the way her granddaughter thinks? Circle clues in the photograph and underline text evidence in the caption that show how she feels.

Write The woman in the photograph is like the librarian and Mary McLeod Bethune because _____

_____

_____

_____

QUICK TIP

In the photograph, I see a grandmother and her granddaughter spending time together. This will help me compare it to text.

In April, it's warm enough for this grandmother to bring her quilting out onto the porch in Gee's Bend, Alabama. Her granddaughter enjoys spending time helping her and learning how to quilt.

Earth

Literature Anthology:
pages 240–253

? How do the diagrams and labels help you understand more about the solar system?

COLLABORATE

Talk About It Look at the diagram on pages 244–245. Talk with a partner about what the diagram shows and helps you understand.

Cite Text Evidence Why does the author include the diagram, heading, and caption? Write text evidence in the chart.

Text Features	How It Helps

CLOSE READING
Tip of the **Week**

When I **reread**, I can use text features to help me understand expository text. I use text evidence to answer questions.

Noah

Write The author uses text features to help me _____

_____

? **How does the author use text and illustrations to help you understand the phases of the Moon?**

Talk About It Reread page 250. Talk with a partner about the diagram and what it shows about the phases of the Moon.

Cite Text Evidence How do the clues in the text, diagram, and caption work together to help you understand the Moon's phases? Use the chart to record evidence.

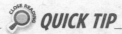 **QUICK TIP**

I can use these sentence frames when we talk about text features.

The diagram and heading help me know that...

The text helps me...

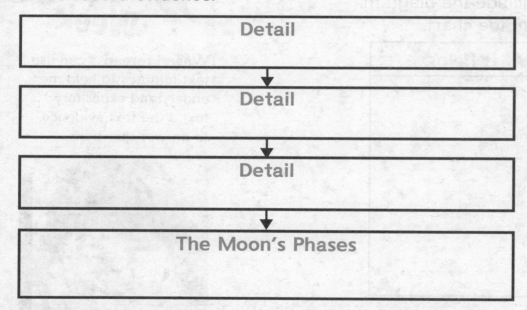

Detail

↓

Detail

↓

Detail

↓

The Moon's Phases

Write The text and diagram work together to help me understand the phases of the Moon because _____

_____

_____

? How does the way the author organizes information help you understand the Moon's surface?

Talk About It Reread page 252. Describe to a partner what the surface of the moon looks like.

Cite Text Evidence How does the author organize the information about the Moon's surface? Write evidence in the chart and tell how it helps you understand the topic.

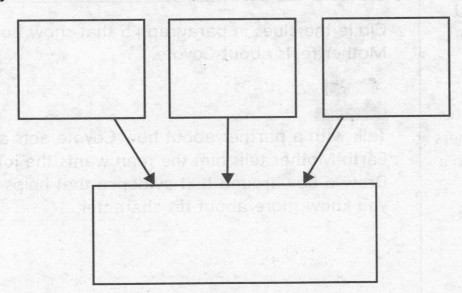

Write I understand about the Moon's surface because the author

_____

_____

_____

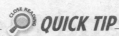

QUICK TIP

When I reread, I can use the way the author organizes information to help me understand the topic.

Your Turn

How does Jeffrey Zuehlke use text features to help you learn more about Earth? Use these sentence frames to organize your text evidence.

Jeffrey Zuehlke uses diagrams and labels to…

He uses illustrations to…

This helps me understand…

Go Digital!
Write your response online.

Coyote and the Jar of Stars

1   A crowd of animals and people gathered in the forest. Coyote shoved his nose between Deer and Owl. "What's going on?" he asked.

2   "Shhh!" scolded Owl. "Earth Mother is speaking."

3   "The sky is empty and dark. Can someone paint pictures in the sky with these stars?" said Earth Mother. She held a large clay jar.

4   "I'll do it!" yelped Coyote, wagging his tail excitedly.

5   Earth Mother frowned. She remembered other times Coyote had helped. He always made a mess of things. She quickly handed the jar of stars to a tall man standing nearby.

6   "Sorry!" she said. "This man wants the job."

7   "People have all the fun!" mumbled Coyote, slinking away.

Reread and use the prompts to take notes in the text.

Reread paragraphs 1–4. Underline the words and phrases the author uses to show you what Coyote is like. List them here:

_____

_____

_____

Circle the clues in paragraph 5 that show how Earth Mother feels about Coyote.

COLLABORATE

Talk with a partner about how Coyote acts after Earth Mother tells him the man wants the job. Draw a box around text evidence that helps you know more about his character.

8   The man dotted the sky with some stars. "This is called Great Bear," he said. After carefully arranging more stars, he said, "This is Mountain Lion." Then he placed the brightest and named it the Morning Star. He put the jar down and gazed upwards.

9   Everyone admired the man's beautiful creations. Earth Mother smiled. No one noticed Coyote tiptoeing through the crowd toward the jar.

10   "I can do better than that," he boasted.

11   Just a few more steps and he'd reach the jar. Coyote was so excited that he didn't notice a pine cone under his feet. He slipped on the pine cone, flipped head over tail, and crashed into the jar of stars! "Yiiii!" Coyote howled.

12   Everyone gasped as the stars floated up and scattered across the sky. They remain there to this day without names or patterns, all because of Coyote. And that's why Coyote looks up and howls at the night sky.

Circle phrases in paragraph 8 that show how the man feels about the work he does. Then circle evidence in paragraph 9 that shows how everyone else feels about his work.

COLLABORATE

Reread paragraphs 10–12. Talk with a partner about what Coyote says to help you understand how he feels. Underline phrases that help you visualize what happens when he tries to help.

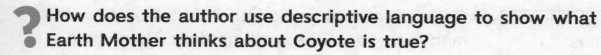 **How does the author use descriptive language to show what Earth Mother thinks about Coyote is true?**

 **QUICK TIP**

When I reread, I can use my annotations to help me understand what characters think and do.

COLLABORATE

Talk About It Reread paragraphs 5 and 11 on pages 84–85. Talk with a partner about how Earth Mother feels about Coyote at the beginning of the story and what happens at the end.

Cite Text Evidence What clues does the author use to help you visualize what happens when Coyote tries to help? Write them in the chart.

What Earth Mother Does	What Coyote Does

Write The author uses descriptive language to show that Coyote

_____

_____

? How is Alexandre Santerne's purpose for creating the photograph similar to the authors' purposes for writing *Earth* and "Coyote and the Jar of Stars"?

COLLABORATE

Talk About It With a partner, discuss what you see in the photograph. Read the caption and talk about why the stars look like trails.

Cite Text Evidence Circle clues in the photograph that help you understand how the planet Earth moves. Then reread the caption and underline how Alexandre Santerne created the photograph.

Write The authors' purposes are like the photographer's purpose because _____

_____

_____

_____

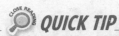

This photograph is called "Star Trails over La Silla." To create it, photographer Alexandre Santerne took many pictures of the stars at night. Then she combined all of the photos into one. The stars look like trails because of Earth's rotation.

Big Ideas from Nature

? How does the way the author compares fish and cars help you to understand how designers solve problems?

Talk About It Reread page 261. Talk with a partner about how designers used fish as inspiration to create a new car's shape.

Cite Text Evidence How does the author describe the problem and solution? Write text evidence in the chart.

Problems	Solutions

Write The author helps me understand how designers solve problems by _____

_____

Literature Anthology: pages 258–267

Tip **of the Week**

When I **reread**, I can identify the way the author organizes information. I find text evidence to answer questions.

Aisha

? **How does the author use photographs and captions to help you understand why shipworms and geckos are important to inventors?**

COLLABORATE

Talk About It Look at the photographs on pages 264 and 265. Turn and talk with a partner how the photographs, labels, and captions help you understand the connection between nature and the invention it inspired.

Cite Text Evidence What clues help you understand why shipworms and gecko feet inspired ways to solve problems? Write clues in the chart.

Photograph Clues	Caption Clues	How It Helps

Write I understand how shipworms and gecko feet are important to inventors because the author _____

_____

_____

CLOSE READING
QUICK TIP

I can use these sentence frames when we talk about how photographs help me understand connections.

The photographs compare...

This helps me understand...

What is the author's purpose for comparing the way birds, fish, locusts, and cars move?

 **QUICK TIP**

When I reread, I can use the way the author compares information to help me understand the topic.

COLLABORATE

Talk About It Reread page 266. Talk with a partner about why designers study the way birds, fish, and locusts move.

Cite Text Evidence What clues does the author use to help you visualize how birds, fish, and locusts are connected to the way cars move? Write them in the chart.

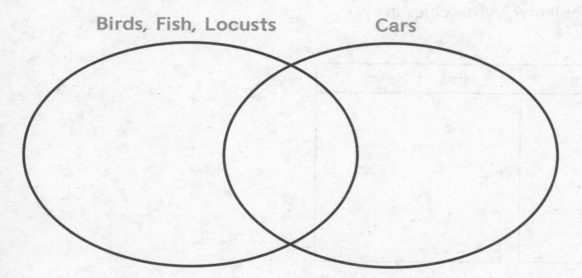

Birds, Fish, Locusts   Cars

Write The author compares birds, fish, locusts, and cars to _____

_____

_____

Your Turn

How does the author organize the text to help you understand that each new idea starts with a problem? Use these sentence frames to organize your text evidence.

The author describes problems to...

Then she compares to help me...

This helps me understand how...

Go Digital!
Write your response online.

Perdix Invents the Saw

1 One day Daedalus heard a knock on his workshop door. "Who's interrupting my work?" he growled. "It's me, Uncle," said his twelve-year-old nephew Perdix (PER-dix). "I want to be a great inventor, too. Will you teach me?"

2 Daedalus's back hurt from chopping firewood. His shoulder ached from sweeping. He didn't really want to teach Perdix. Then he got an idea. "If you do all the chores, I'll let you watch me invent things," he said.

3 Perdix did the chores, cooked meals, and observed how Daedalus worked. The boy had some clever ideas. He wanted to make a smaller ax for cutting branches for firewood. Daedalus disagreed. "Just leave the inventing to me," he always hissed.

Reread and use the prompts to take notes in the text.

Reread paragraph 1 and find a clue that helps tell what might happen later in the story. Write it here:

_____

_____

In paragraph 2, circle the chores that Daedalus needs to do. Then underline why he wants to trick Perdix.

COLLABORATE

Reread paragraph 3. Talk with a partner about how you know what kind of character Perdix is. Make a mark in the margin beside the clues.

4 One afternoon Perdix roasted a large fish for lunch. After eating, Daedalus licked his fingers and smacked his lips. "That was pretty good, Perdix, but I've eaten better," he said.

5 Perdix sighed and started washing the dishes. In the process he cut his finger on the jagged backbone of the fish. He held the backbone up and studied its sharp edges. "I can imitate this design and make a fine tool for cutting wood," he thought.

6 The next day, Perdix sawed all the firewood before Daedalus awoke. "How did you finish your work so early?" Daedalus snarled.

7 "It was easy with my new invention," said Perdix. He showed his uncle the saw.

8 Daedalus was reluctant to praise his clever nephew. "It should be my invention because you cooked that fish for me," he sniffed.

9 Perdix just smiled. He now realized that he was a great inventor, too.

Reread paragraphs 5–7. Circle clues that help you understand how Perdix got his idea. Then underline how his new invention made his life better.

COLLABORATE

Talk with a partner about what Daedalus thinks of Perdix's saw. What clues in paragraph 8 help you understand how he feels? Draw a box around them.

How do you know how Perdix feels about his invention? Make a mark beside the clue and write it here:

_____

_____

? **How do the author's clues in the beginning of the myth help you predict what might happen to Perdix at the end?**

COLLABORATE

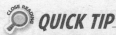**QUICK TIP**

When I reread, I can use clues the author gives me to help me make predictions.

Talk About It Reread paragraphs 1 on pages 91–92. Turn and talk with a partner about how you knew that Perdix might invent something by the end of the myth.

Cite Text Evidence What clue at the beginning of the myth helps you figure out that Perdix would invent something? Write text evidence in the chart.

Text Evidence	How It Helps

Write The author's clues at the beginning of the myth helped me make a prediction by _____

_____

? How is the way the poet organizes her poem like the way the authors organize the text in *Big Ideas From Nature* and "Perdix Invents the Saw."

COLLABORATE

Talk About It Read "What Is Pink?" Talk with a partner about what the poem is about and how it is organized.

Cite Text Evidence Circle phrases the poet repeats. Think about how the poet describes each color. Underline clues that tell where each color can be found.

Write The way the poet organizes her poem is like what the authors did because _____

_____

_____

_____

QUICK TIP

I notice how the poet organizes the information in her poem. This will help me compare it to the selections I read this week.

What Is Pink?

What is pink? A rose is pink
By a fountain's brink.
What is red? A poppy's red
In its barley bed.
What is blue? The sky is blue
Where the clouds float through.
What is white? A swan is white
Sailing in the light.
What is yellow? Pears are yellow,
Rich and ripe and mellow.
What is green? The grass is green,
With small flowers between.
What is violet? Clouds are violet
In the summer twilight.
What is orange? Why, an orange,
Just an orange!

— Christina Rossetti

Riding the Rails West!

? How does the way the author organizes the text help me understand why people wanted to go west by train?

Literature Anthology: pages 272–275

COLLABORATE

Talk About It Reread the first two paragraphs on page 273. Talk with a partner about what caused people to use trains and why railroads were built to connect the whole country.

Cite Text Evidence What clues does the author use to help you understand the cause and effect structure? Write text evidence in the chart.

Tip of the Week

When I **reread**, I can use how the author organizes the information. I look for text evidence to answer questions.

Cause	→	Effect

Write The author organizes the text to help me understand _____

_____

Micco

? How does the sidebar help you understand how important trains are today?

COLLABORATE

Talk About It Reread the sidebar on page 275. Talk with a partner about how the sidebar helps you understand how trains are used today.

Cite Text Evidence How is the information in the sidebar different from what you read in the selection? Find examples in the text.

Riding the Rails West!	Sidebar

Write The author uses the sidebar to help me understand that

_____

_____

_____

 **QUICK TIP**

I can use these sentence frames when I talk about the sidebar.

The information in the sidebar...

The author includes it to help me...

Your Turn

How does the way the author organizes information help you understand how important trains are to our history? Cite evidence from the text using these sentence frames.

The author organizes information by...

She also uses a sidebar to...

This helps me see that...

Go Digital!
Write your response online.

Discovering Life Long Ago

1　In the past, people wrote in diaries and journals. They wrote letters to friends and families. They also wrote autobiographies to tell their life stories. Diaries, journals, and autobiographies tell us what people thought and felt. They also give details about daily life in the past. They describe the food people ate. They tell what kind of transportation they used.

2　Posters, newspapers, and old photographs also give details about events in the past. So do speeches and songs. Photographs show people's clothes and how they had fun.

3　Both words and pictures from the past help us see how people lived long ago. They tell a history of people, places, and things. They take us back in time.

Reread and use the prompts to take notes in the text.

Reread paragraphs 1 and 2. Underline the ways people use to tell about the way life was long ago. In the margin, number the different things we can learn. List three of them here:

_____

_____

_____

COLLABORATE

Turn and talk with a partner about how the author organized the information in this selection. Circle the paragraph that summarizes all the information.

? **How does the author help you understand how people learn about events in the past?**

Talk About It Reread paragraphs 1 and 2 on page 97. Talk with a partner about the ways people learn more about the past.

Cite Text Evidence How does the author arrange the information to help you understand how we learn about life long ago? Write text evidence here.

Paragraph 1	Paragraph 2	This Helps Because...

Write The author helps me understand how people learn about the past by _____

_____

QUICK TIP

When I reread, I can use the way the author shares information to help me understand the topic better.

? How do the song lyrics help you visualize an event in history in the same way the words and phrases in "Riding the Rails West!" and "Discovering Life Long Ago" do?

Talk About It Read the song lyrics. Talk with a partner about what Betsy and her brother did.

Cite Text Evidence Circle words and phrases in the song lyrics that tell who went on the journey and what creatures they brought with them. Underline clues that show what they did.

Write The song lyrics help me visualize the journey by _____

_____

_____

_____

QUICK TIP

I can use the lyrics to help me visualize what is happening. This will help me compare the song to the selections I read this week.

from Sweet Betsy from Pike

Oh, do you remember sweet
  Betsy from Pike,
Who crossed the wide prairies
  with her brother Ike?
With two yoke of oxen, a
  big yaller dog,
A tall Shanghai rooster and
  one spotted hog. . . .

They camped on the prairie for
  weeks upon weeks.
They swam the wide rivers and
  crossed the tall peaks.
And soon they were rollin' in
  nuggets of gold.
You may not believe it but
  that's what we're told.

American Folk Song
Adapted by Merrill Staton

The Real Story of Stone Soup

? What do the narrator's words and actions tell you about his character?

COLLABORATE

Talk About It Reread page 280. Talk with a partner about what the narrator says about paying the Chang brothers.

Cite Text Evidence What phrase helps you know what the narrator is like? Write it here and explain how it helps.

Text Evidence	How It Helps

Write The narrator's words help me see that the narrator is _____

_____

_____

Literature Anthology pages 278–295

CLOSE READING

Tip of the Week

When I **reread**, I can use what the characters say to understand what they do. I look for text evidence to answer questions.

Lizzie

? **How does the author show that the narrator is wrong about how smart the boys are?**

Talk About It Reread the last three paragraphs on page 283. Talk about what the Chang brothers do.

Cite Text Evidence What evidence helps you see that the boys are smart? Write it here and tell what it shows about the brothers.

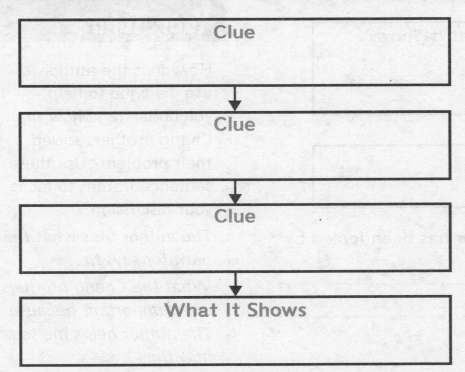

Clue

Clue

Clue

What It Shows

Write I know the narrator is wrong about the brothers because

_____

_____

 **QUICK TIP**

I can use these sentence frames when we talk about what the brothers do.

The author uses what the Chang brothers say to...

This shows that they...

How do you know that the narrator has been fooled by the Chang brothers?

Talk About It Reread the last two paragraphs on page 289. Talk with a partner about what the narrator says about the sesame oil.

Cite Text Evidence What do the characters say that shows that the narrator has been fooled? Use the chart to write text evidence.

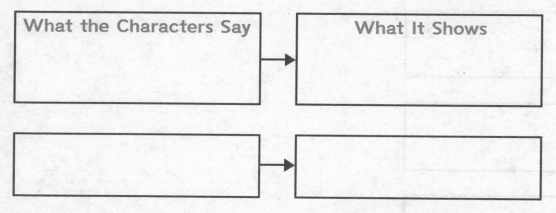

What the Characters Say	What It Shows

Write The author helps me see that the narrator has been fooled by

_____

_____

Your Turn

How does the author use dialogue to help you understand how the Chang brothers solved their problem? Use these sentence frames to focus your discussion.

The author uses what the narrator says to...

What the Chang brothers say is important because...
The author helps me see how they...

Go Digital!
Write your response online.

Healthful Food Choices

Food Is Energy

1   What's for dinner? There are so many choices. Every time you go to the market you find a variety of foods to eat. Which ones do you choose? Why does it matter what you eat?

2   It matters because you move around and think all day long. You go to school. You play with friends. You do chores and homework. All that activity takes energy. You get energy from the food you eat. You need to eat energy-producing food because, unlike a plant, your body can't make its own food.

Reread and use the prompts to take notes in the text.

In paragraph 1, underline how the author gets you interested in reading more.

Reread paragraph 2. Circle how the author explains why it matters what you eat.

COLLABORATE

Talk with a partner about why "Food is Energy" is a good heading for this section. Make a mark in the margin beside text evidence that supports your answer. Write it here.

_____

_____

3 The next time you go to the market, what will you buy? You might choose a juicy red tomato for two reasons. It's healthful and delicious, and it's good for you, too. It gives you energy!

Recipe for Easy Salsa

Use a tomato to make a healthful snack. Try this recipe! Ask an adult to help.

What You Need

1 large tomato
¼ red onion
½ cup cilantro
½ lime
salt
hot sauce

1 Chop tomato, onion, and cilantro.

2 Place the chopped vegetables in a small bowl.

3 Squeeze the lime juice into the bowl.

4 Add a little bit of salt and hot sauce.

5 Mix everything together with a spoon.

Enjoy your salsa with baked corn chips!

Reread paragraph 3. Underline the three reasons why you might buy a tomato.

COLLABORATE

Reread the recipe. Talk with a partner about how the recipe shows that making good choices is important. Circle clues in the recipe that show examples of healthful food choices.

? **What is the author's purpose for including his recipe for salsa?**

COLLABORATE

Talk About It Reread the recipe on page 104. Talk with a partner about the ingredients that go into making salsa.

Cite Text Evidence What clues show that the recipe is a good example of how to make healthful choices? Write text evidence.

Text Evidence	What It Tells Me

Write The author includes the recipe for salsa because _____

_____.

 **QUICK TIP**

When I reread, I can use text features to help me understand the author's purpose.

Integrate

How does the poet help you understand the importance of making good choices in the same way the authors do in *The Real Story of Stone Soup* and "Healthful Food Choices"?

COLLABORATE

Talk About It Read the poem. Talk with a partner about what the vulture can do to feel better.

Cite Text Evidence Circle what happens to the vulture in the poem. Underline why those things happen. Then draw a box around what the vulture can do to change things.

Write The poet and the authors help me understand the importance of making good choices by _____

_____

_____

_____

_____

QUICK TIP

I read in the poem that the vulture has a choice to make. This will help me compare the poem to the selections I read this week.

The Vulture

The Vulture eats between
   his meals,
And that's the reason why
He very, very, rarely feels
As well as you and I.

His eye is dull, his head
   is bald,
His neck is growing thinner.
Oh! what a lesson for us all
To only eat at dinner!

— Hilaire Belloc

The Talented Clementine

? How does the author help you understand how Margaret's teacher and Mrs. Rice are different?

Literature Anthology
pages 300–317

COLLABORATE

Talk About It Reread paragraphs 3 and 4 on page 306. Turn to your partner and talk about what Margaret's teacher and Mrs. Rice do.

Cite Text Evidence What do Margaret's teacher and Mrs. Rice do and say that show how they are different? Write text evidence here.

CLOSE READING

Tip of the Week

Clues	How They Are Different

When I **reread**, I can use what the characters say and do to help me understand how they feel. I look for text evidence to answer questions.

Write I know that Margaret's teacher and Mrs. Rice are different

_____

_____

Jamie

? **How does the author use humor to describe how important Clementine is to the talent show?**

COLLABORATE

Talk About It Reread the first four paragraphs on page 313. Talk about how Clementine describes what's happening on stage.

Cite Text Evidence What words and phrases show that what happens is funny? Write evidence and tell how that helps you see how important Clementine is to the show.

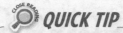**QUICK TIP**

I can use these sentence frames when we talk about how the author uses humor.

The author describes what happens in a funny way because...

I read that Clementine...

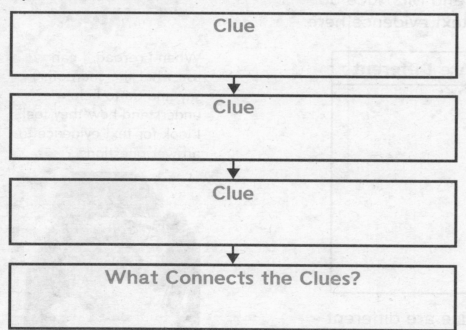

Clue

⬇

Clue

⬇

Clue

⬇

What Connects the Clues?

Write The author uses humor to _____

_____

? **How does the author help you understand what Principal Rice means when she tells Clementine that she is "one of a kind"?**

COLLABORATE

Talk About It Reread the last two paragraphs on page 316. Talk about what Principal Rice says to Clementine and how it makes her feel.

Cite Text Evidence What clues help you understand what "one of a kind" means? Write text evidence in the chart.

Text Evidence	How It Helps

Write I understand what "one of a kind" means because the author

_____

_____

_____

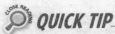 **QUICK TIP**
When I reread, I can use nearby words and phrases to help me understand what the author means.

Your Turn

How does the author use what the characters do and say to help you understand how Clementine has changed? Use these sentence frames to focus your discussion.

The author describes Clementine...

She uses dialogue to tell me that her teachers...

I can see how Clementine has changed because the author...

Go Digital!
Write your response online.

Clementine and the Family Meeting

 QUICK TIP

When I reread, I can use the author's words and phrases to help me understand how the characters feel.

? How does the author help you understand how Clementine feels about the family meeting?

COLLABORATE

Talk About It Reread page 321. Discuss with your partner why you think Clementine is nervous about the family meeting.

Cite Text Evidence What words and phrases help you understand how Clementine feels? Write text evidence in the chart.

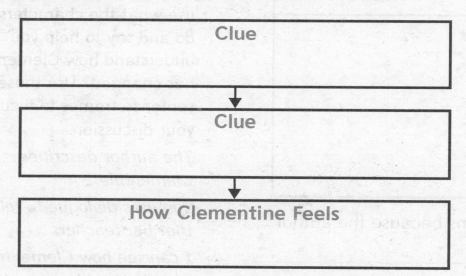

Clue

↓

Clue

↓

How Clementine Feels

Write The author helps me understand how Clementine feels by

_____

_____

_____

? How does the author use illustrations to help you understand how Clementine feels?

COLLABORATE

Talk About It Look at the illustration on page 323. Turn to a partner and talk about what it shows you about how Clementine feels.

Cite Text Evidence What clues in the illustration help you understand how Clementine feels? Write them here.

Clues	How Clementine Feels

Write The illustration helps me understand how Clementine feels

_____

_____

QUICK TIP

I can use these sentence frames when we talk about the illustration.

The illustration shows Clementine...

This helps me understand that she feels...

? **How do you know how Clementine feels about having a new baby in the family?**

COLLABORATE

Talk About It Reread paragraph 3 on page 324. Talk about what Clementine says.

Cite Text Evidence What words and phrases help you know how she feels about having a new baby in the family? Write them here.

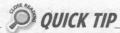

QUICK TIP
I can use what the characters do and say to help me understand how they feel.

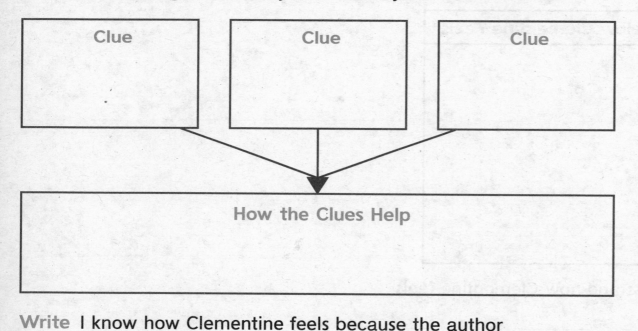

Clue	Clue	Clue

How the Clues Help

Write I know how Clementine feels because the author _____

_____

_____

QUICK TIP

I use what I see in the photograph to understand the theme. This will help me compare it to text.

? How does the photographer and the author of *The Talented Clementine* show how you can use what you know to help others?

COLLABORATE

Talk About It Look at the photograph and read the caption. With a partner, talk about what the girls are doing.

Cite Text Evidence Circle details in the photograph that show what each girl's talent is. Then underline the text evidence in the caption that tells what they are doing. In the margin next to the photograph, tell how the girls feel. Underline evidence in the photograph that supports your answer.

Write The photographer and the author help me understand _____

_____

_____

_____

_____

Janey and Lucretia practice one hour a day. They are performing in a talent show and want to win.

Amazing Wildlife of the Mojave

? How does the author use words and phrases to help you visualize how the chuckwalla protects itself?

Literature Anthology: pages 326–337

COLLABORATE

Talk About It Reread page 329. Talk with a partner about how the chuckwalla protects himself.

Cite Text Evidence What words does the author use to describe what the chuckwalla does to protect itself? Write text evidence in the chart.

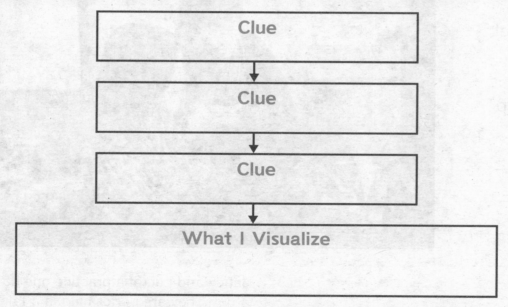

Clue

↓

Clue

↓

Clue

↓

What I Visualize

Write I can visualize how the chuckwalla protects itself because

_____

_____

CLOSE READING
Tip of the **Week**

When I **reread,** I can use the author's words and phrases to help me visualize. I look for text evidence to answer questions.

Luke

? **How does the author help you understand how light-colored and dark-colored animals survive in the desert?**

COLLABORATE

Talk About It Reread page 331. Talk with a partner about why "Light Colors Help" is a good heading for this section.

Cite Text Evidence What text evidence shows how animals survive in the Mojave desert? Write it in the chart.

Light-colored animals	Dark-colored animals

Write The author helps me understand how light-colored and dark-colored animals survive by _____

_____.

QUICK TIP

I can use these sentence frames to help me when we talk about animals in the desert.

In this section, the author describes...

It helps me understand that animals...

? **How does the author feel about the iguana's ability to change color?**

COLLABORATE

Talk About It Reread the second paragraph on page 336. Talk with a partner about how the author describes what iguanas do.

Cite Text Evidence What clues help you see how the author feels about what iguanas can do? Write evidence to support your answer.

Text Evidence	How the Author Feels

Write I know how the author feels about iguanas because _____

_____

_____.

QUICK TIP

When I reread, I can use the author's words and phrases to help me understand his point of view.

Your Turn

How do you know how the author feels about the wildlife in the Mojave desert? Use these sentence frames to organize your text evidence.

The author says that living in the desert is...

He tells about how the animals...

This helps me know that he feels...

Go Digital!
Write your response online.

Little Half Chick

1 Once in Mexico, an unusual chick hatched. He had only one eye, one wing, and one leg. He was named Little Half Chick. He quickly learned to hop faster on one leg than most chickens could walk on two. He was a curious and adventurous chick and soon grew tired of his barnyard environment. One day he decided to hop to Mexico City to meet the mayor.

2 Along the way, he hopped by a stream blocked with weeds. "Could you clear these weeds away so my water can run freely?" the stream gurgled. Little Half Chick helped the stream. Then he hopped on.

3 It started to rain. A small fire on the side of the road crackled, "Please give me shelter from this rain, or I will go out!" Little Half Chick stretched out his wing to protect the fire until the rain stopped.

Reread and use the prompts to take notes in the text.

In the first paragraph, circle words and phrases that describe Little Half Chick.

Write them here:

_____

_____

_____

COLLABORATE

Reread paragraphs 2 and 3. Talk with a partner about what Little Half Chick does to help the stream and the rain. Underline text evidence.

4   Further down the road Little Half Chick met a wind that was tangled in a prickly bush. "Please untangle me," it whispered. Little Half Chick untangled the wind. Then he hopped on to Mexico City.

5   Little Half Chick did not meet the mayor. He met the mayor's cook. She grabbed him, plunged him into a pot of water, and lit a fire. However, the fire and the water remembered Little Half Chick's kindness. The fire refused to burn, and the water refused to boil. Then, the grateful wind picked him up and carried him safely to the top of the highest tower in Mexico City.

6   Little Half Chick became a weather vane. His flat body told everyone below the direction the wind blew. And he learned this lesson: Always help someone in need because you don't know when you'll need help.

Reread paragraph 4. Circle how Little Chick helps the wind.

COLLABORATE

Reread paragraphs 5 and 6. Talk with a partner about what happens to Little Half Chick when he meets the mayor's cook. Underline words and phrases that describe what happens.

How does Little Half Chick escape the pot of water? Make marks in the margin beside the text evidence. Write it here.

_____

_____

_____

? **What words and phrases help you visualize how Little Half Chick escapes the cook's pot of water?**

Talk About It Reread the third paragraph on page 118. Turn and talk with a partner about how Little Half Chick escapes.

Cite Text Evidence What words and phrases help you picture what happens? Write text evidence in the chart.

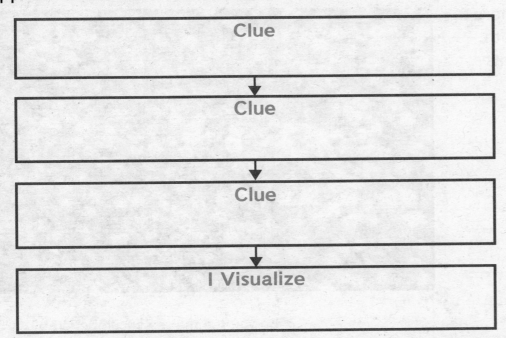

Clue

Clue

Clue

I Visualize

Write The author helps me visualize how Little Half Chick escapes by

_____

_____

QUICK TIP

I can use these sentence frames when we talk about Little Half Chick.

The author says that...

The words and phrases in the folktale help me picture...

? How does this photograph and the photographs and illustrations in *Amazing Wildlife of the Mojave* and "Little Half Chick" help you understand how animals adapt to challenges?

COLLABORATE

Talk About It Look at the photograph and read the caption. Talk with a partner about what you see.

Cite Text Evidence Circle the sea cucumber crab. Now draw a circle about the same size somewhere on the sea cucumber. Compare what's inside both circles. Think about what the photographer wants you to know.

Write Photographs and illustrations help me understand _____

_____

_____

_____

_____

QUICK TIP

I see that the photographer is helping me understand how crabs protect themselves. This will help me compare the photograph to text.

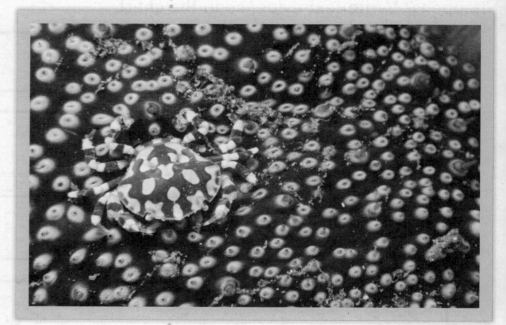

Do you see the sea cucumber crab? He's there. He's resting on a sea cucumber. These crabs use camouflage to protect themselves from animals that want to eat them.

Hot Air Balloons

? How does the author help you visualize what a balloon launch is like?

COLLABORATE

Talk About It Reread the second paragraph on page 344. Turn and talk with a partner about what a hot air balloon launch is like.

Cite Text Evidence What words and phrases help you picture a balloon launch? Write text evidence in the chart.

Text Evidence	What I Visualize

Write I can visualize what a balloon launch is like because the author

_____

_____

Literature Anthology:
pages 342–355

Tip of the **Week**

When I **reread**, I can think about how the author uses words and phrases. I look for text evidence to answer questions.

Mina

? **How does the author organize the text to help you understand how a pilot flies a hot air balloon?**

Talk About It Reread page 353. Talk with a partner about how the pilot controls where the hot air balloon goes.

Cite Text Evidence What clues help you understand how a pilot controls a hot air balloon? Write text evidence in the chart.

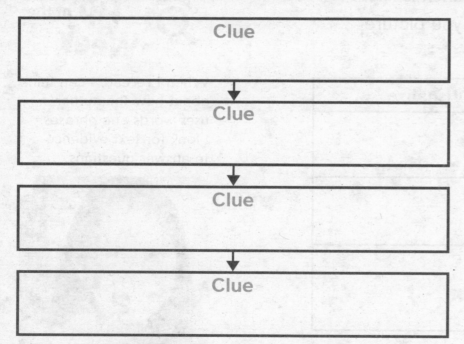

Clue
Clue
Clue
Clue

Write The author organizes the text to show _____

_____

_____

QUICK TIP

I can use these sentence frames when we talk about how the author organizes information.

I read that the pilot...

The author then explains that...

? **How does the author use words and phrases to help you see how hot air balloons move?**

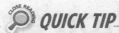 **QUICK TIP**

When I reread, I look for words and phrases the author uses to help me understand the topic.

COLLABORATE

Talk About It Reread the second paragraph on page 354. Talk with a partner about how wind and currents help hot air balloons fly.

Cite Text Evidence What words does the author use to help you understand how hot air balloons use currents? Write text evidence.

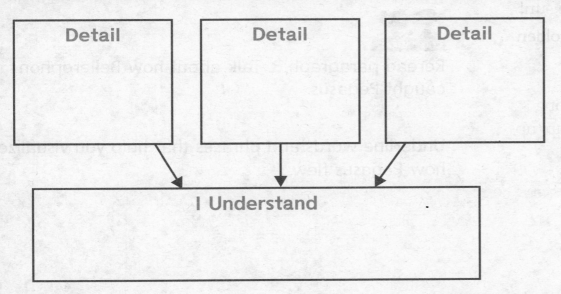

| Detail | Detail | Detail |

I Understand

Write The author helps me understand how hot air balloons move by

_____

_____

Your Turn

How does the way the author organizes the text in this selection help you understand how people are able to fly? Use these sentence frames to focus your discussion.

The author helps me understand how hot air balloons fly by...

She also uses words and phrases to...

The way the text is organized helps me...

Go Digital!
Write your response online.

Bellerophon and Pegasus

1   Bellerophon worried about his task. How could one man stop the Chimera? He asked the goddess Athena for help. In a dream, she showed him where to find the flying horse Pegasus.

2   Bellerophon woke up from the dream holding a golden bridle. It shone as brightly as the sun!

3   Bellerophon caught Pegasus with the golden bridle and leaped onto the creature's back. Pegasus snorted and stamped his hooves. He stretched his mighty wings with a strong motion. Then he carried his new master up, up, up, into the sky. They were in flight!

Reread and use the prompts to take notes in the text.

In paragraph 1, circle how you know that Bellerophon is worried about what he has to do. Write the text evidence here:

_____

_____

COLLABORATE

Reread paragraph 3. Talk about how Bellerophon caught Pegasus.

Underline words and phrases that help you visualize how Pegasus flew.

4   Bellerophon and Pegasus soared and circled above the countryside as they hunted the Chimera. At last they found the dreadful beast.

5   The monster's heads roared and hissed so loudly that the ground shook. Fire shot from the monster's mouths. Pegasus flew swiftly around the Chimera, swooping down and away. Again and again the monster lunged at the flying horse and his rider. Each time it missed them. Bellerophon swung his sword with all his might, three times. The monster fell.

6   Bellerophon and Pegasus flew back to King Iobates. To prove his victory, Bellerophon brought King Iobates a strand of lion's mane, a snake's scale, and a goat's horn from the Chimera. At last King Iobates agreed to let Bellerophon marry his daughter. Everyone in the kingdom was invited to the wedding feast. And Pegasus got a golden bucket filled with the finest oats in the land.

Reread paragraphs 4 and 5. Circle words that describe the Chimera.

How does the author describe what Pegasus does when they found the Chimera? Underline text evidence. Write it here:

_____

_____

COLLABORATE

Reread paragraph 6. Talk with a partner about what Bellerophon brings back to King Iobates. Draw a box around each item.

Make a mark in the margin beside the sentence that helps you see that Pegasus did a great job.

? **How does the author help you visualize how Bellerophon and Pegasus defeat the Chimera?**

COLLABORATE

Talk About It Reread paragraph 5 on page 125. Talk with a partner about how Bellerophon and Pegasus battle the Chimera.

Cite Text Evidence What words and phrases help you picture the action? Write text evidence in the chart.

Details

↓

What I Visualize

Write The author helps me visualize the battle by _____

_____

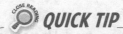

QUICK TIP

I can use these sentence frames when we talk about how the author describes the action in the story.

The author uses vivid words to tell how Bellerophon and Pegasus...

I use the author's words to picture...

? How does the way the photographer organizes the information in the photograph and the way the authors organize text in *Hot Air Balloons* and "Bellerophon and Pegasus" help you see how people fly?

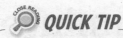

COLLABORATE

Talk About It Look at the photograph and read the caption. Talk with a partner about what the pilot, photographer, and surfer are doing. Choose one of the images and discuss what the photographer wants you to know.

Cite Text Evidence Draw a line to separate the two things that are happening in the photograph. Then draw a circle around the reason why the photographer is flying.

Write The photographer and authors use organization to _____

_____

_____

_____

_____

This helicopter pilot and the photographer have a birds-eye view of a big wave surfer in Hawaii. Not only are they watching him surf, but the photographer is also filming him.

The Winningest Woman of the Iditarod Dog Sled Race

? How does the poet help you understand how the narrator feels about finishing the Iditarod?

COLLABORATE

Talk About It Reread page 361. Talk with a partner about what the Iditarod was like.

Cite Text Evidence What words and phrases show how the narrator feels about finishing the race? Write text evidence in the chart.

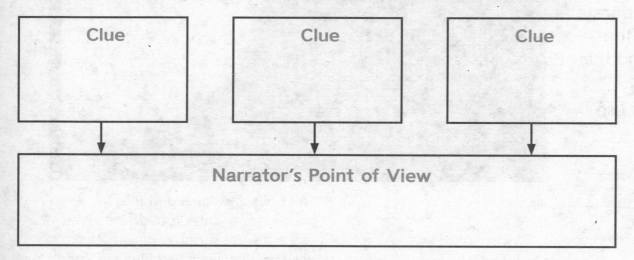

Clue	Clue	Clue

Narrator's Point of View

Write The poet helps me understand how the narrator feels by

_____

_____

Literature Anthology: pages 360–362

Tip of the Week

When I **reread**, I can think about how the poet uses words and phrases. I look for text evidence to answer questions.

Juan

The Brave Ones

QUICK TIP

I can use these sentence frames when we talk about word choice.

The poet repeats...

This helps me...

? How does the poet's use of repetition in "The Brave Ones" help you visualize what it is like to fight a fire?

COLLABORATE

Talk About It Reread page 362. Talk with a partner about how the poet's words and phrases make you feel.

Cite Text Evidence What words and phrases does the poet repeat? Write them in the chart.

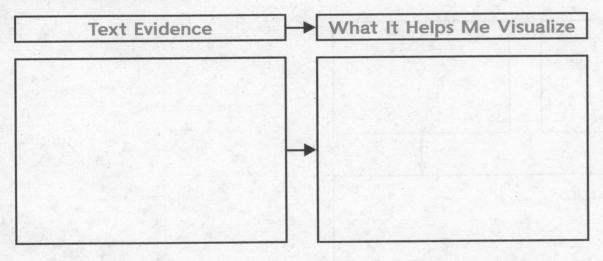

Text Evidence	→	What It Helps Me Visualize
	→	

Write The poet repeats words and phrases to help me visualize by

_____

_____

_____

Your Turn

How do the poets use repetition to help you understand the message in their poems? Use these sentence frames to organize your text evidence.

In "The Winningest Woman of the Iditarod Dog Sled Race" the poet repeats words to...

The poet of "The Brave Ones" uses repetition to... These words help me understand the theme of each poem by...

Go Digital!
Write your response online.

Narcissa

? **How does the poet use words and phrases to help you visualize what Narcissa is doing?**

Talk About It Reread the second stanza on page 365. Turn and talk with a partner about what Narcissa is doing.

Cite Text Evidence What words and phrases help you picture in your mind what Narcissa is doing? Write text evidence in the chart.

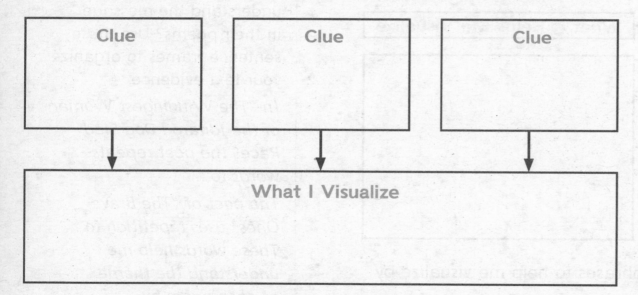

Clue	Clue	Clue

What I Visualize

Write I can visualize what Narcissa is doing because _____

_____

QUICK TIP

When I reread, I can use the poet's words and phrases to help me visualize what a character is doing.

? **Why does the author repeat the words "as still" at the end of the poem?**

COLLABORATE

Talk About It Reread the third and fourth stanzas on page 365. Talk with a partner about what Narcissa is doing and how she is changing.

Cite Text Evidence What clues help you understand why the poet repeats the words "as still"? Write text evidence in the chart.

Text Evidence	What It Shows

Write The author repeats the words "as still" to _____

_____ .

QUICK TIP

I can use these sentence frames when we talk about how the poet uses repetition.

I read that Narcissa is...

The poet wants me to know that...

? **How is the way the photographer shares his message like the way the poets do in "The Winningest Woman of the Iditarod Dog Sled Race," "The Brave Ones," and "Narcissa"?**

COLLABORATE

Talk About It Look at the painting and read the caption. Talk with a partner about what the grandmother and her grandchildren are doing.

Cite Text Evidence Circle details in the photograph that show two ways the grandchildren are being inspired. Underline evidence in the caption that gives you more information about what is going on.

Write The photographer and poets share their messages by _____

_____

_____

_____

_____

_____

_____

QUICK TIP
I see details in the photograph that show how people are inspired. This will help me compare the photograph to text.

June is an artist. She teaches art on the weekends and loves to visit the art museum. She also loves to take her grandchildren with her to talk about new paintings on display.

Clever Jack Takes the Cake

? How does the way the author repeats words and phrases help you understand Jack's character?

Literature Anthology:
pages 366–383

COLLABORATE

Talk About It Reread the fifth paragraph on page 369. Talk with a partner about what Jack is doing.

Cite Text Evidence What words does the author repeat? Write text evidence and explain how it helps you understand what Jack is like.

Tip of the Week

Text Evidence	Jack

When I **reread**, I can use words and phrases to help me understand more about the character. I look for text evidence to answer questions.

Write The author uses repetition to help me understand that Jack is

_____

_____

Olivia

? **How does the author use language to help you visualize what the bear is doing?**

COLLABORATE

Talk About It Reread page 377. Talk with your partner about what the bear does.

Cite Text Evidence What words and phrases help you visualize what happens to Jack's cake? Write text evidence in the chart.

Text Evidence	What I Visualize

Write The author uses words and phrases to help me visualize _____

_____

_____

QUICK TIP

I can use these sentence frames when we talk about the author's word choice.
The author uses words and phrases to...

This helps me visualize...

? **How does the illustration help you understand Jack's story?**

Talk About It Reread page 380 and look at the illustration on page 381. Talk with a partner about the parts of Jack's story.

Cite Text Evidence What clues in the illustration help you understand what Jack tells the princess? Write clues in the chart.

Illustration Clues	How It Helps

Write The author uses the illustration to help me see that Jack

_____

_____

QUICK TIP
When I reread, I can use illustrations to help me understand more about the story.

Your Turn

How does the author use text and illustrations to show how Jack accomplishes his goal? Use these sentence frames to organize your text evidence.

The author describes how Jack...

Illustrations help me see...

This helps me know that Jack...

Go Digital!
Write your response online.

When Corn Was Cash

Native Americans

1   In the past, Native Americans often used the barter system. People from different families and villages got together to exchange items. They traded crops such as corn, beans, and tobacco. They exchanged dried fish and meat. They traded stones for making arrowheads and animal hides for making clothes.

2   Native Americans in the Northeast valued beads made from quahog clamshells. The beads were called wampum. *Wampum* means "strings of white shell beads" in the Algonquian language. Native Americans used wampum in ceremonies. They gave it as gifts.

3   Later, when Native Americans began trading with colonists from Europe, wampum even became a form of money.

Reread and use the prompts to take notes in the text.

In paragraph 1, underline how the author helps you understand what the barter system is. Write it here:

_____

_____

Circle the words and phrases in paragraph 2 that the author uses to help you visualize what wampum looks like.

COLLABORATE

Talk with a partner about how wampum was used. Make marks in the margin beside text evidence that supports your discussion.

Settlers and Traders

[4] In the 1600s, people from Europe started coming to America. Life was hard for these immigrants. They had very little money. Unlike today, there were not many stores.

[5] Colonists relied on bartering to survive. They exchanged cloth from Europe for crops that the Native Americans grew. They also traded beaver furs, baskets of coal, and cows.

[6] Later, the colonies used corn and rice and other goods as money. Some especially valuable items were accepted as a form of payment throughout the colonies.

In paragraph 4, underline how the author shows that life in the 1600s was different from today.

COLLABORATE

Reread paragraphs 5 and 6. Talk with a partner about how the colonists bartered for what they needed. Circle what they used to barter with.

Make a mark beside the statement that shows how important bartering was to the colonists.

? How does the author show how the colonists used bartering to survive?

COLLABORATE

Talk About It Reread the excerpt on page 137. Talk with a partner about how the colonists bartered to get what they needed.

Cite Text Evidence How do you know how important bartering was to the colonists? Write text evidence in the chart.

Text Evidence	What It Means

Write The author shows how the colonists used bartering to survive

_____

_____

QUICK TIP

As I reread, I can find text evidence to help me answer questions.

How do the poet and the author of *Clever Jack Takes the Cake* help you visualize how the characters meet their needs?

COLLABORATE

Talk About It Read the poem. Talk with a partner about how the animals in the poem get what they need.

Cite Text Evidence Circle clues in the poem that show that there are plenty of nuts. Underline how the animal gets what it needs.

Write I can visualize how Jack and the animal in the poem get what they need because _____

_____

_____

_____

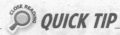

QUICK TIP

In the poem, the animal finds a way to get what it needs. This will help me compare the poem with a story I read this week.

Here's a Nut

Here's a nut, there's a nut;
Hide it quick away,
In a hole, under leaves,
To eat some winter day.
Acorns sweet are plenty,
We will have them all:
Skip and scamper lively
Till the last ones fall.

— Louisa May Alcott

Bravo, Tavo!

Literature Anthology:
pages 390–409

? How does the author use dialogue to help you understand Tavo and Papa's problems?

COLLABORATE

Talk About It Reread page 393. Turn to a partner and discuss how Tavo feels.

Cite Text Evidence What do Tavo and Papa say that helps you know what their problems are? Write text evidence in the chart.

CLOSE READING

Tip of the Week

When I **reread**, I can think about how the author uses dialogue. I look for text evidence to answer questions.

Tavo		Papa	
What He Says	What It Means	What He Says	What It Means

Jayla

Write The author uses dialogue to help me understand _____

_____

_____

? **How does the illustration help you understand Tavo's new problem?**

COLLABORATE

Talk About It Look at the illustration on page 401. Talk about what it shows about Tavo's new problem.

Cite Text Evidence What clues in the illustration show Tavo's new problem? Write the clues in the chart.

Clues	How It Helps

Write The illustration helps me understand that _____

_____

_____

 **QUICK TIP**

I can use these sentence frames when we talk about Tavo's problem.

The illustration shows...

The illustration helps me understand...

? **How does the author's word choice help you visualize what happens at the end of the story?**

COLLABORATE

Talk About It Reread page 409. With a partner, discuss the conversation between Tavo and his father.

Cite Text Evidence What words and phrases help you visualize what happens at the end of the story? Write text evidence in the chart.

Descriptive Language	→	What I Visualize

Write The author uses words to help me visualize _____

_____

_____

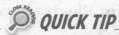 **QUICK TIP**

When I reread, I can use the author's words and phrases to help me better understand the characters and events in a story.

Your Turn

How does the author help you understand how Tavo's problems are connected to his father's problems? Use these sentence frames to organize your text evidence.

The author uses descriptive words to...

He uses dialogue to...

This helps me understand that...

Go Digital!
Write your response online.

Trash into Art

Alexander Calder's Giant Mobiles

1   In the 1950s, the sculptor and artist Alexander Calder had a big problem. He wanted to build gigantic mobiles (MOH-beelz) from metal. A mobile is a moving sculpture. It hangs from a ceiling. It sways and moves when people touch it. Most metals were much too heavy to move the way Calder wanted.

2   Calder solved his problem by recycling aluminum from the bodies of old airplanes. The aluminum came in large sheets. It was easy to cut into interesting shapes. And it was light enough to move quickly. Calder reused the old metal to create his huge moving sculptures.

Reread and use the prompts to take notes in the text.

Underline the sentence that shows Alexander Calder's problem. Then circle how he solved his problem. Write his problem and solution here.

Problem: _____

_____

Solution: _____

_____

COLLABORATE

Reread paragraph 2. Talk with a partner about why Calder recycled old airplanes. Make marks in the margin beside the text evidence that supports your discussion.

Miwa Koizumi's Sea Creatures

[3]   When artist Miwa Koizumi came to New York City, she saw empty plastic bottles everywhere. Plastic bottles overflowed from trash cans. They littered the streets. She decided to use some of these bottles in her art.

[4]   Today Koizumi cuts and melts the plastic bottles into shapes. Then she attaches the shapes to each other to create forms that look like sea animals. She hangs them so that they seem to be swimming. Koizumi changes bits of old plastic into fantastic floating sea creatures.

[5]   To Koizumi, finding art materials in the trash was only natural. People have hunted for materials to reuse since ancient times. Even animals reuse bits of junk. Birds build nests with old scraps of fabric and discarded materials. Why shouldn't artists search around outside for art materials?

In paragraph 3, circle why Miwa Koizumi decided to use plastic bottles to make art.

Reread paragraph 4. What steps does Miwa Koizumi take to make her art? Number the steps from 1 to 3 in the margin.

COLLABORATE

Reread paragraph 5. Talk with a partner about how the author feels about reusing trash to create art. Underline the text evidence and write it here:

_____

_____

_____

? **How does the author feel about using trash to create art?**

COLLABORATE

Talk About It Reread the excerpts on pages 143–144. Talk with a partner about how the author feels about using trash as art.

Cite Text Evidence How does the author tell how he feels about recycling trash into art? Write text evidence in the chart.

Text Evidence	Author's Point of View

Write The author's point of view about using trash to create art is

_____

_____

_____

QUICK TIP

I can use the author's words and phrases to help me understand how he feels about recycling trash into art.

? How is the house in the photograph like Tavo's sneakers in *Bravo, Tavo!* and the art in "Trash into Art"?

COLLABORATE

Talk About It Look at the photograph and read the caption. Talk with a partner about what the house is made of.

Cite Text Evidence Circle clues that show what the house is made of. Underline evidence in the caption that helps you understand how the house was made.

Write The house in the photograph is like Tavo's sneakers and the art made from trash because _____

_____

_____

_____

_____

_____

_____

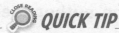
QUICK TIP

I see a house made out of bottles. This will help me compare text to photography.

In 1980, a man who lived on Prince Edward Island in Canada collected 12,000 bottles from people, stores, and restaurants in his community. He used them to build this bottle house.

Wildfires

Literature Anthology:
pages 416–427

? How does the author use text features to help you understand how wildfires start?

COLLABORATE

Talk About It Reread pages 418–419. Turn to a partner and talk about the text features the author uses.

Cite Text Evidence How do the text features help you understand how wildfires start? Write evidence in the chart and tell how they help you understand the content.

Tip of the Week

When I **reread**, I can use text features to help me understand the topic. I look for text evidence to answer questions.

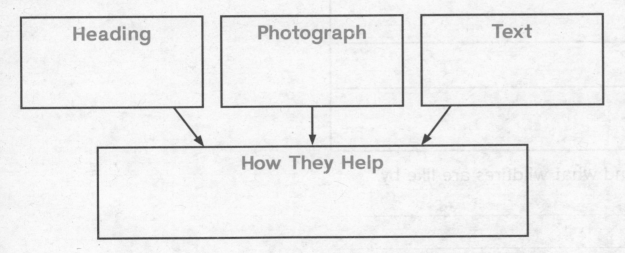

Heading	Photograph	Text

↓ ↓ ↓

How They Help

Sebastián

Write I understand how wildfires start because the author uses _____

_____

_____

? **How does the author help you understand what wildfires are like?**

COLLABORATE

Talk About It Reread page 423. Talk with a partner about what you learned from the real-world example.

Cite Text Evidence What details from the real-world example help you understand more about wildfires? Write your evidence in the chart.

Text Evidence	What I Understand

Write The author helps me understand what wildfires are like by

_____

_____

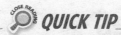

I can use these sentence frames when we talk about wildfires.

The author tells about...

This helps me understand...

? How does the author help you visualize what happens after a wildfire stops burning?

COLLABORATE

Talk About It Reread paragraphs one and two on page 425. Discuss with a partner what happens to a forest after a wildfire.

Cite Text Evidence What words and phrases help you understand what a forest is like after a wildfire? Write text evidence in the web.

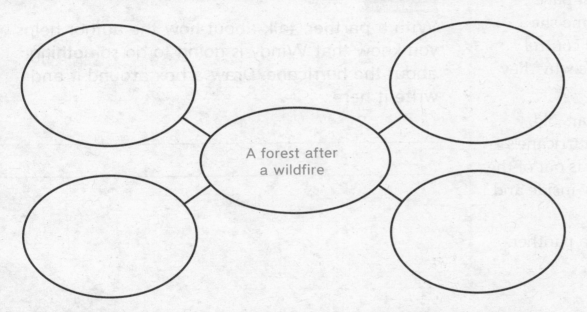

A forest after a wildfire

Write I can visualize what happens after a wildfire stops burning because the author _____

_____

Your Turn

How do the text features and the way Seymour Simon organizes information help you understand more about wildfires? Use these sentence frames to organize your thoughts.

Seymour Simon uses photographs and captions to...

He organizes the text by...

This helps me understand that wildfires...

Go Digital!
Write your response online.

Windy Gale and the Great Hurricane

1   Once, in Florida, a baby girl was born. That night was so windy that all the mountains blew away. Only the flat land we call the Everglades was left. Well, some of that wind must have blown into that baby girl. From the time she was knee-high to a tadpole, she could control the wind with her breath alone. That's why they called her Windy Gale.

2   One day when Windy was nine years old, a warning sounded on the radio. "A hurricane's a-comin'! We can't stop it! Prevention is out of the question, folks. You'll just have to stay inside and wait it out!"

3   Windy called Gusty, her pet Florida panther.

Reread and use the prompts to take notes in the text.

In paragraph 1 underline the sentence that explains how Windy Gale got her name.

How does the author help you visualize the night Windy was born? Circle text evidence.

COLLABORATE

With a partner, talk about how the author helps you know that Windy is going to do something about the hurricane. Draw a box around it and write it here:

_____

_____

4   Windy said, "I don't believe for one windy minute that we should just wait out this storm! It'll hit Miami soon, and I need you to run me there fast!" She jumped on Gusty's back.

5   Gusty gave a roar. Then he ran so fast that he arrived a clear two minutes before he even left.

6   The hurricane was zooming up the Gulf. Windy knew just what to do to stop it. She took three BIG breaths, 1. . . 2. . . 3. . . and sucked the wind right out of that hurricane.

Reread the excerpt. Underline two examples of exaggeration in the paragraphs. Write those examples here.

1. _____

2. _____

COLLABORATE

Talk with a partner about why the author uses exaggeration in the tall tale.

_____

_____

? How does the author help you visualize what Windy Gale can do?

COLLABORATE

Talk About It Reread the excerpts on pages 150 and 151. Turn and talk with a partner about what Windy Gale can do.

Cite Text Evidence What words and phrases help you picture what Windy Gale can do? Write text evidence in the chart.

Text Evidence	What I Visualize

Write The author helps me visualize what Windy Gale can do by

_____

_____

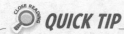 **QUICK TIP**

When I reread, I can use the author's descriptive words to help me visualize.

? **How is the way the artist uses cause and effect in the painting like the way the authors use cause and effect in *Wildfires* and "Windy Gale and the Great Hurricane"?**

COLLABORATE

Talk About It Look at the painting and read the caption. Then talk with a partner about what you see happening in the painting and how the people are working together.

Cite Text Evidence Circle clues in the painting that show why the people are working together. Underline what they are doing. Then draw a box around why the title of the painting is a good title.

Write The artist and authors use cause and effect to _____

_____

_____

_____

_____

QUICK TIP

In the painting, I see a dark, stormy sky and people working. This will help me compare text to art.

This painting was originally created by American artist Olof Krans in 1939. It is an oil painting called "It Will Soon Be Here."

Elizabeth Leads the Way:
Elizabeth Cady Stanton and the Right to Vote

Literature Anthology:
pages 432–449

? How does the author use what Elizabeth says and does to help you understand her personality?

COLLABORATE

Talk About It Reread pages 436–437. Turn to a partner and talk about what Elizabeth Cady Stanton says and does.

Cite Text Evidence What does Elizabeth say and do? Write evidence in the chart and tell how it helps you understand what she is like.

Text Evidence	Elizabeth

Write The author uses what Elizabeth says and does to help me understand that _____

_____

Tip of the **Week**

When I **reread**, I can think about how the author describes what a character says and does. I look for text evidence to answer questions.

Camilla

? **How do you know that Elizabeth felt strongly about what she believed in?**

COLLABORATE

Talk About It Reread page 445. Talk with a partner about what Elizabeth thinks about a woman's right to vote.

Cite Text Evidence What words help you understand how strong Elizabeth's feelings are? Write text evidence in the chart.

Text Evidence	How Elizabeth Feels

Write I know that Elizabeth felt strongly about her beliefs because the author _____

_____

_____

QUICK TIP

I can use these sentence frames when we talk about Elizabeth.

The author uses words and phrases to tell that Elizabeth believes...

This helps me understand that she feels...

? **How does the author help you understand how Elizabeth's ideas changed America?**

COLLABORATE

Talk About It Reread page 449. Talk with a partner about what the author says about Elizabeth.

Cite Text Evidence What words and phrases show how Elizabeth changed America? Write text evidence in the chart.

Text Evidence	What It Means
How It Helps	

Write The author helps me understand how Elizabeth changed America by _____

_____

QUICK TIP

When I reread, I can use words and phrases to help me understand how Elizabeth helped change America.

Your Turn

How does Tanya Lee Stone use Elizabeth's biography to teach you about what it means to be a good citizen? Use these sentence frames to organize your text evidence.

Tanya Lee Stone tells that Elizabeth...

She shows how Elizabeth...

This helps me understand...

Go Digital!
Write your response online.

Susan B. Anthony Takes Action!

1 Susan Brownell Anthony was born in Massachusetts in 1820. Her family believed that all people are equal. At the time Susan was born, however, this idea of equality was very unusual. Men and women did not have the same rights. Women could not vote and they could not own property. Life was different for Susan. She learned to read and write at the age of three, even though she was a girl.

Reread and use the prompts to take notes in the text.

Circle words and phrases that help you understand what equality is. Write them here:

_____

_____

COLLABORATE

Talk with a partner about how life was different for Susan. Underline text evidence in the excerpt.

Women Get the Vote!

1   Susan gave as many as 100 speeches around the country every year for forty-five years. She always stayed excited and hopeful about her work.

2   Not everyone agreed with her ideas. Susan and her friend Elizabeth Cady Stanton had to fight hard for many years for the rights of all people. They always did their work peacefully. It was not until fourteen years after Susan died that women in the United States were allowed to vote. The long struggle would not have been successful without the work of Susan B. Anthony.

In paragraph 1, underline clues that help you visualize what Susan was like. Write them here:

_____

_____

COLLABORATE

Reread paragraph 2. Talk with a partner about how other people felt about her ideas. What did Susan and Elizabeth do? Circle words and phrases that show what they did.

Make a mark beside the sentence that shows how the author feels about Susan.

? **How does the author help you know how she feels about Susan B. Anthony?**

COLLABORATE

Talk About It Reread paragraph 2 on page 158. Talk about what the author says about Susan.

Cite Text Evidence What words help you know how the author feels about Susan and the work she did? Write text evidence in the chart.

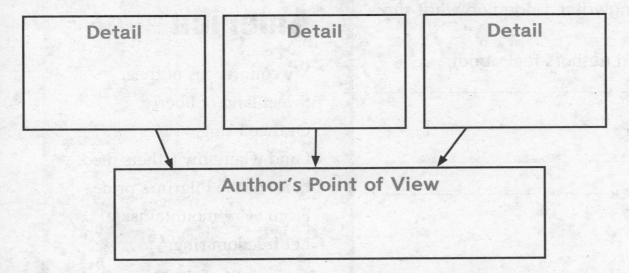

Detail	Detail	Detail

Author's Point of View

Write The author helps me know how she feels about Susan B. Anthony by _____

_____

_____

QUICK TIP

When I reread, I can use the author's words and phrases to understand her point of view.

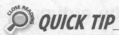

? How do you know how the songwriter and authors of *Elizabeth Leads the Way* and "Susan B. Anthony Takes Action" feel about America?

COLLABORATE

Talk About It Read the song lyrics. Talk with a partner about how the songwriter feels about America.

Cite Text Evidence Circle words and phrases in the lyrics that show what America means to the songwriter. Underline what the writer says about freedom.

Write I know how the songwriter and authors feel about America because _____

_____

_____

QUICK TIP The lyrics help me understand how the writer feels. This will help me compare the song to the selections I read this week.

America

My country 'tis of thee,
Sweet land of liberty,
Of thee I sing.
Land where my fathers died,
Land of the Pilgrim's pride,
From ev'ry mountainside
Let freedom ring.

—Music by Henry Carey
—Words by Samuel F. Smith

It's All in the Wind

? How does the author help you understand how strong wind can be?

Talk About It Reread "Wind is Energy" on page 457. Turn to a partner and talk about what the wind can do.

Cite Text Evidence What words describe the wind and how strong it is? Write text evidence in the chart.

Text Evidence	What I Understand

Write I understand how strong wind can be because the author _____

_____

Literature Anthology: pages 456–459

CLOSE READING

Tip of the Week

When I **reread**, I can think about the how the author uses words and phrases. I look for text evidence to answer questions.

William

? **How does the author use text features to help tell what windmills do?**

COLLABORATE

Talk About It Look at the text features on page 458. Talk with a partner about how a wind machine works.

Cite Text Evidence How do the text features help you understand more about wind machines? Write text evidence in the chart.

Text Features	Clues	How It Helps

Write The author uses text features to help me _____

_____

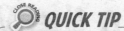
QUICK TIP

When I **reread**, I can think about how the text features help me understand the topic better.

Your Turn

How does the author show that wind energy is important? Use these sentence frames to help you organize text evidence.

The author helps me understand wind by...

This helps me see that it is important by...

Go Digital!
Write your response online.

Power for All

1.   Every day, students in many countries are in a race against the Sun. Many don't have electricity. For this reason, they must do their homework during the daylight hours or use dangerous oil lamps or candlelight at night.

2.   In Tsumkwe (CHOOM-kwee), a small town in Namibia, Africa, villagers were lucky. Until recently, they got all their electricity from a generator powered by oil. However, there were problems with the generator. It cost a lot of money. And it only produced electricity for three hours each day.

Reread and use the prompts to take notes in the text.

In paragraph 1, why does the author say that students must race against the Sun? Underline text evidence that answers that question. Write it here:

_____

_____

Circle the words in paragraph 2 that help you know where Tsumkwe is located.

COLLABORATE

Talk with a partner about the problems with the generator. Make marks in the margin to show text evidence to support your discussion.

? How does the author's word choice help you visualize life without electricity?

COLLABORATE

Talk About It Reread the excerpt on page 163. Turn and talk with a partner about what life was like in Tsumkwe, Africa.

Cite Text Evidence What words and phrases help you visualize what life would be like without electricity? Write text evidence in the chart.

Text Evidence	What I Visualize

Write The author helps me visualize what life would be like without electricity by _____

_____

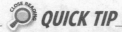
QUICK TIP
When I reread, I can think about how the author uses words and phrases to help me visualize.

? How does the painting and the photographs and illustrations in "It's All in the Wind" and "Power for All" help you understand the different kinds of energy?

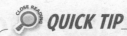

QUICK TIP
I see how wind works in the painting. This will help me compare text to art.

COLLABORATE

Talk About It Look at the painting and read the caption. With a partner, discuss how the boat is moving.

Cite Text Evidence Circle clues in the painting that show what makes the ship move. Underline details that help you understand that the schooner is moving.

Write The painting, photographs, and illustrations help me understand about energy because _____

_____

_____

_____

_____

This oil painting of an American schooner was painted sometime during the 19th century by an unknown artist.

King Midas and the Golden Touch

? How does the author help you visualize how much King Midas loves gold?

COLLABORATE

Literature Anthology: pages 462–475

Talk About It Reread pages 464 and 465 and look at the illustration. With a partner, talk about what King Midas does.

Cite Text Evidence What words, phrases, and images help to show how King Midas feels about gold? Write text evidence in the web.

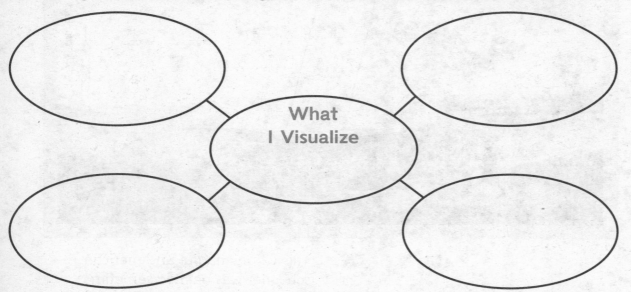

What I Visualize

Write I can picture how much Midas loves gold because the author

_____

_____

CLOSE READING

Tip of the Week

When I **reread**, I can think about the characters' words and actions to help me understand the theme of the story. I look for text evidence to answer questions.

Holly

? **How does the author show that King Midas is not just interested in gold?**

QUICK TIP

I can use these sentence frames when we talk about King Midas.

The author describes how King Midas...

This tells me that he feels...

COLLABORATE

Talk About It Reread page 468. Talk with a partner about the gift that King Midas gives Marigold.

Cite Text Evidence What clues help you see that King Midas is interested in more than his money? Write text evidence in the chart.

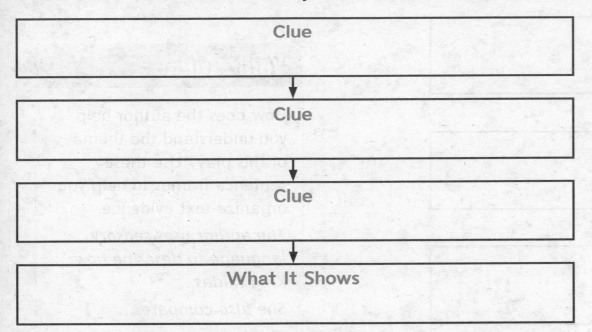

Clue

↓

Clue

↓

Clue

↓

What It Shows

Write The author shows that King Midas cares about other things by

_____

_____

How does the author show that something might happen to Marigold later in the story?

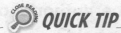 **QUICK TIP**

When I reread, I can use the author's words and phrases to predict that something might happen later in the story.

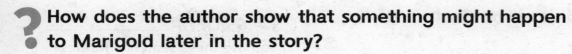
COLLABORATE

Talk About It Reread page 471. Talk with a partner about what happens to the stone and the rose.

Cite Text Evidence What clues show that something might happen to Marigold? Write text evidence.

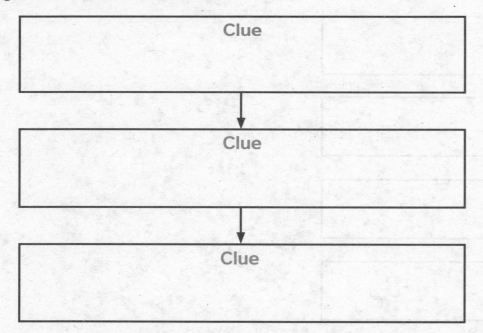

Clue

↓

Clue

↓

Clue

Write I know that something might happen to Marigold because

_____

_____

Your Turn

How does the author help you understand the theme of this play? Use these sentence frames to help you organize text evidence.

The author uses sensory language to describe how King Midas...

She also compares...

This helps me understand the theme because...

Go Digital!
Write your response online.

Carlos's Gift

1   Carlos wanted a puppy in the worst way. He dreamed about puppies—big ones, little ones, spotted ones, frisky ones. Now it was his birthday, and Carlos had one thing on his mind. A puppy! When Mama handed him a flat, square box, Carlos almost started to cry.

2   It was a book about caring for dogs.

3   Papa smiled, "You need to learn how to care for a puppy before you get one."

4   Carlos read the book that night. He found a photograph of the exact kind of bulldog puppy that he craved. He eagerly showed Mama the next morning.

Reread and use the prompts to take notes in the text.

Underline phrases in paragraph 1 that show how much Carlos wanted a puppy. Circle clues that show how he feels when Mama gives him his present. Write text evidence here:

_____

_____

_____

COLLABORATE

Reread paragraph 4. Talk with a partner about what Carlos does. Draw a box around two phrases that show how Carlos feels about learning to care for a dog.

1   Carlos started working at the shelter on Saturday. His assignment was sweeping. Afterwards, the dogs scampered out to play. One dog named Pepper had a funny curly tail that never stopped wagging. She was fully grown but as playful as a puppy. When Pepper leaped in the pile of stick and leaves that Carlos had just swept up, he laughed.

2   Carlos went to the shelter every weekend. He began to treasure his time with the dogs, especially Pepper. One day Carlos asked why Pepper was still at the shelter.

3   Miss Jones sighed, "We've had trouble finding a home for Pepper. Most people don't want such an energetic dog."

4   Carlos suddenly realized he didn't want a bulldog puppy. He wanted Pepper. "I wish I could buy her," he replied.

In paragraph 1, draw a box around words and phrases that describe Pepper. Underline the text evidence in paragraph 3 that tells why Pepper has not found a home. Write it here:

_____

_____

COLLABORATE

Reread the rest of the excerpt. Talk with a partner about what Miss Jones and Carlos say about Pepper. Circle text evidence to support your discussion.

How does the author use dialogue to show how Carlos feels about Pepper?

COLLABORATE

Talk About It Reread paragraphs 2–4 on page 170. Talk with a partner about how Carlos reacts to what Miss Jones says.

Cite Text Evidence What does Carlos think and say about Pepper? Write text evidence in the chart.

Text Evidence	How Carlos Feels

Write I know how Carlos feels about Pepper because the author uses dialogue to _____

_____

? How does the photographer show what's important in the same way the authors do in *King Midas and the Golden Touch* and "Carlos's Gift"?

COLLABORATE

Talk About It Look at the photograph and read the caption. Talk with a partner about what you see happening in the photograph.

Cite Text Evidence Circle clues that show why Craig is helping Jason. Underline what Craig is doing in the photograph and caption. Draw a box around the part of the photograph that helps you know how Craig feels.

Write The photographer shows what's important by

_____

_____

_____

QUICK TIP

I can see in the photograph what one boy feels is important. This will help me compare it with the stories I read this week.

When Jason broke his leg, Craig carried his books and helped him get around school.

Nora's Ark

Literature Anthology: pages 482–501

 How does the author hint that something is going to happen later in the story?

COLLABORATE

Talk About It Reread the last seven paragraphs on page 485. Talk with a partner about what is happening.

Cite Text Evidence What words and phrases hint that there is going to be a flood? Write text evidence in the chart.

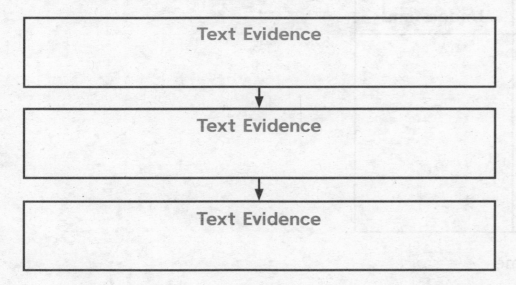

Text Evidence

↓

Text Evidence

↓

Text Evidence

Write I know that something is going to happen because the author _____

_____

_____

Tip of the Week

CLOSE READING

When I **reread**, I can think about how the author uses words and phrases. I look for text evidence to answer questions.

Harrison

? **How does the author use illustrations to help you understand what is happening during the flood?**

Talk About It Reread page 491 and look at the illustration. Turn and talk with a partner about what the illustration shows.

Cite Text Evidence What clues in the illustration help you better understand what a flood is like? Write evidence in the chart.

Illustration Clues	Text Evidence	What I Understand

Write The author uses illustrations to help me _____

_____

_____

? **What words and phrases help you visualize what Grandma is like?**

COLLABORATE

Talk About It Reread page 495. Talk with a partner about why Grandma doesn't want Wren to go with her.

Cite Text Evidence What words and phrases describe Grandma's character? Write text evidence in the chart.

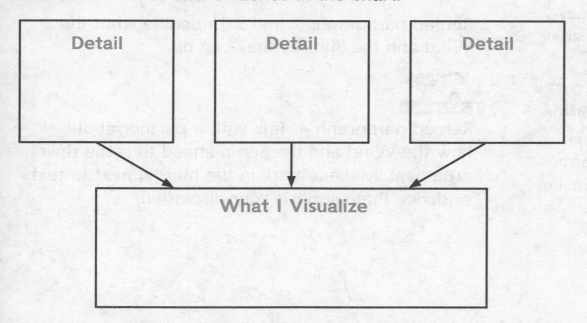

| Detail | Detail | Detail |

What I Visualize

Write The author helps me visualize what Grandma is like by

_____

_____

_____

QUICK TIP

When I reread, I can use words and phrases to help me understand what characters do.

Your Turn

How does what the author says about Wren and her grandmother at the beginning of the story help you understand the message? Use these sentence frames to organize your text evidence.

At the beginning of the story, the author...

She uses illustrations to...

This helps me understand...

Go Digital!
Write your response online.

The Wind and the Sun

[1]   The Wind and the Sun both lived in the sky. Like most neighbors, they got along much of the time. However, sometimes they argued about who was the strongest.

[2]   "I am stronger than you!" boasted the Wind one day. "I can topple trees and flatten homes. On a sunny day, I can spoil the weather conditions by blowing in clouds and rain."

[3]   The Sun smiled, "No! I am stronger. I provide daylight and the heat that keeps people warm."

[4]   "Let's have a contest to determine who is stronger," blustered the Wind. "See that farmer down there in his field? We'll each try to make him take off his coat. Whoever succeeds is the winner."

Reread and use the prompts to take notes in the text.

In paragraph 1, circle what the Wind and the Sun argued about. Write it here:

_____

_____

Reread paragraphs 2 and 3. Underline what the Wind and the Sun say they can do.

COLLABORATE

Reread paragraph 4. Talk with a partner about how the Wind and the Sun planned to settle their argument. Make a mark in the margin next to text evidence that supports your discussion.

5   "Okay, you go first," the Sun agreed.

6   The Wind took a big breath and blew and blew. He tried to blast away the farmer's coat with all his strength, but the farmer only pulled his coat tighter.

7   "*Brr!* That's peculiar," said the farmer. "The weather forecast on the radio didn't predict a freezing wind for today."

8   Soon the Wind grew tired and stopped howling. "Your turn, Sun," he panted.

9   Sun nodded and smiled. He sent out his warmest rays.

10   The farmer began to sweat as he labored in the field. "Ah, it certainly has become a warm, sunny day," he sighed with relief as he removed his coat. And with that, the Sun won the contest.

11   *Gentle persuasion works better than force.*

Underline words and phrases in paragraph 6 that tell what the Wind does to make the farmer take off his coat.

Circle words and phrases in paragraph 9 and 10 that tell what the Sun does to make the farmer take off his coat.

COLLABORATE

Talk with a partner about what the Sun and the Wind do. Then reread the last line. Use text evidence to support the moral of the story. Write it here:

_____

_____

_____

_____

? **How does the author use what the characters say and do to tell the theme or moral of the story?**

Talk About It Reread the excerpt on page 177. Talk with a partner about how the Sun and the Wind talk to each other.

Cite Text Evidence How does what the characters say and do show that the moral of the story is a good one? Write text evidence in the chart.

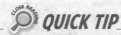

QUICK TIP

I can reread to find text evidence that supports the theme of the story.

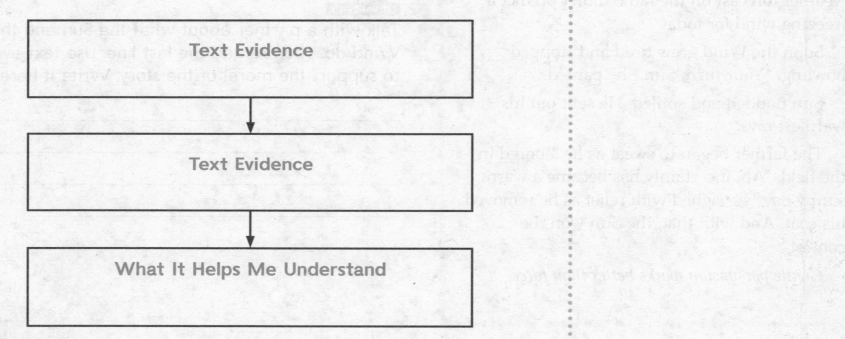

Text Evidence

Text Evidence

What It Helps Me Understand

Write I understand the moral of the story because the author _____

_____

_____

_____

? How is the way the artist illustrates the theme similar to the way the author shows the themes in *Nora's Ark*?

COLLABORATE

Talk About It Look at the painting and read the caption. Talk with a partner about how weather affects the train and people.

Cite Text Evidence Circle clues in the painting that show how weather affects people. Underline how the artist portrays the theme of working together.

Write The artist illustrates the same theme as in the story I read this week by _____

_____

_____

_____

_____

This is a Currier and Ives print of people clearing the tracks for a steam engine after a snowstorm.

Out of This World!
The Ellen Ochoa Story

? How does the author use text features to help you understand Ellen Ochoa's biography?

COLLABORATE

Talk About It Look at the text features on pages 507–509. Discuss with a partner what you learned about Ellen Ochoa.

Cite Text Evidence What do the text features help you understand? Write text evidence in the chart.

Text Feature	What It Tells Me about Ellen Ochoa
quotation	
caption	
photograph	

Write Text features help me understand _____

_____

_____

Literature Anthology:
pages 506–515

CLOSE READING
Tip of the Week

When I **reread**, I can use text features such as quotations, photos, and captions to help me learn more about Ellen Ochoa.

Yusuf

How does the author use photographs and captions to help you understand that goals are important?

QUICK TIP

When I reread, I can see that the photos and captions provide additional information about the main ideas in the story.

COLLABORATE

Talk About It Reread the second paragraph on page 508. Turn and talk with a partner about Ellen's dream.

Cite Text Evidence What clues in the photographs and captions show how Ellen reached her goals? Write text evidence.

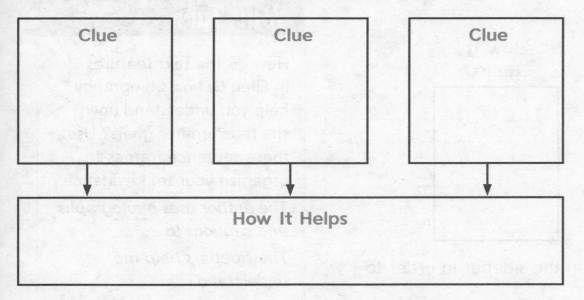

Clue	Clue	Clue

How It Helps

Write The author uses photographs and captions to show how Ellen Ochoa reached her goals by _____

_____

_____

_____

? **How does the sidebar help you understand Ellen Ochoa's career?**

COLLABORATE

Talk About It Reread the sidebar on page 515. Talk to a partner about the information included in the sidebar.

Cite Text Evidence What can you infer about Ochoa's trips based on the information in the sidebar and the information you learned in the text?

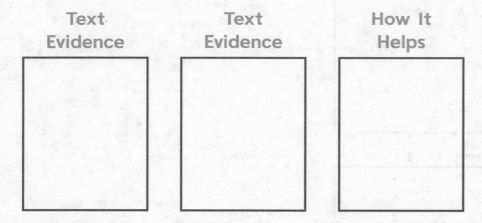

Text Evidence	Text Evidence	How It Helps

Write The author includes the information in the sidebar in order to

_____

_____

QUICK TIP

When I reread, I can use text features to help me understand the topic.

Your Turn

How do the text features in Ellen Ochoa's biography help you understand how she reached her goals? Use these sentence frames to organize your text evidence.

The author uses photographs and captions to...

The sidebars help me understand...

I know Ellen Ochoa reached her goals because the author...

Go Digital!
Write your response online.

A Flight to Lunar City

[1] Going to the Moon had been Maria's goal since she was five. The dream had motivated Maria to enter a science project in the National Space Contest. She had invented Robbie, the robot dog, as her science project. He was the perfect Moon pet. Maria and Robbie had won first prize —a trip to Lunar City, the first settlement on the Moon.

[2] Now they were almost there! Robbie wriggled and squirmed. "Settle down!" Maria scolded. Sometimes Robbie was awfully wild, like a real puppy. Maria was thinking about adjusting his Personality Profile Program to make him a little calmer.

Reread and use the prompts to take notes in the text.

Underline words and phrases in paragraphs 1 and 2 that help you understand the setting of the story. Describe the setting here.

_____

_____

COLLABORATE

Talk with a partner about Maria's goal. Circle text evidence to support your discussion. Write those details here.

_____

_____

_____

1   Just then Robbie jumped out of Maria's arms and leaped across the landing ship. He jumped onto the stick with all four paws and growled fiercely. He tugged and chewed on it. "Stop!" cried Maria.

2   All at once the control stick shifted into position. The lights came back on. The landing ship whooshed forward. "Robbie, you did it!" laughed Commander Buckley. "Good dog!" She handed Robbie back to Maria. "Now we can land on the Moon."

3   Maria smiled proudly. Robbie was the best robot dog ever!

Reread paragraph 1. Underline words and phrases that describe what Robbie does. Circle what Maria says.

COLLABORATE

Reread paragraphs 2 and 3. Talk with a partner about how Robbie solves the problem. Draw a box around details in the story that let you know how Commander Buckley and Maria feel. Write how they feel here.

_____

_____

? **How does the author use details to help you visualize how Robbie fixed the problem?**

COLLABORATE

Talk About It Reread the excerpt on page 184. Talk with a partner about what Robbie does.

Cite Text Evidence What words and phrases show what Robbie does to fix the problem? Write text evidence in the chart.

Text Evidence	What I Visualize

Write I can visualize what Robbie does because the author _____

_____

_____

When I reread, I can use the author's words and phrases to help me visualize what characters do.

? How is the message of this song similar to Ellen Ochoa's path to becoming an astronaut in *Out of This World!* and Maria's goals in "A Flight to Lunar City"?

COLLABORATE

Talk About It Read the song lyrics. With a partner, talk about how you feel after reading it.

Cite Text Evidence Underline words and phrases in the lyrics that tell what the song's message is. Think about how the message makes you feel.

Write The message of this song is similar to Ellen Ochoa's career path because _____

_____

_____

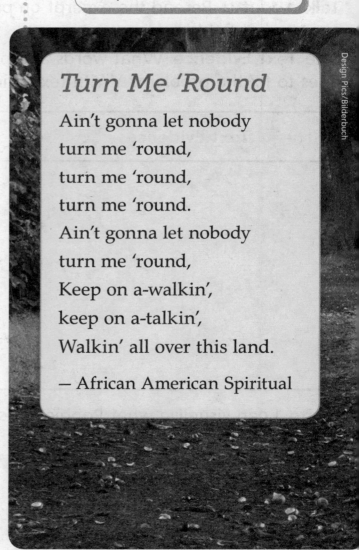

Turn Me 'Round

Ain't gonna let nobody

turn me 'round,

turn me 'round,

turn me 'round.

Ain't gonna let nobody

turn me 'round,

Keep on a-walkin',

keep on a-talkin',

Walkin' all over this land.

— African American Spiritual

Design Pics/Bilderbuch

Alligators and Crocodiles

? How does the author use maps to help you compare and contrast alligators and crocodiles?

COLLABORATE

Talk About It Look at the maps on pages 526 and 527. Talk with a partner about how the two maps are different.

Cite Text Evidence What clues on the maps show how alligators and crocodiles are alike and different? Write text evidence.

Text Evidence	Map Clues

Write The author uses the maps to help me compare and contrast alligators and crocodiles by _____

_____

Literature Anthology: pages 520–541

CLOSE READING

Tip of the **Week**

When I **reread**, I can use maps to help me compare and contrast. I look for text evidence to help me answer questions.

Collin

How does the author use diagrams to help you understand how alligators and crocodiles are alike and different?

Talk About It Reread pages 528 and 529. Look at the diagrams.
Talk with a partner about why the diagram labels are different colors.

Cite Text Evidence What clues in the diagrams help you to compare and contrast alligators and crocodiles? Write text evidence.

COLLABORATE

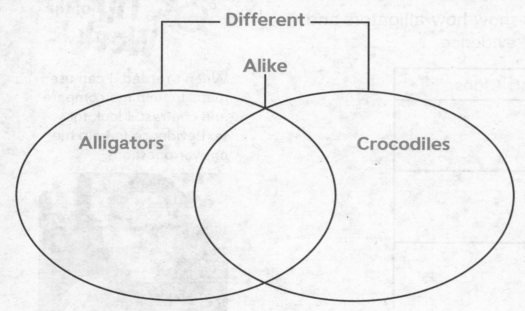

Different

Alike

Alligators   Crocodiles

Write The author uses diagrams to help me compare and contrast alligators and crocodiles by _____

_____

? How does the author organize the information to help you understand the animals' nests?

COLLABORATE

Talk About It Reread page 536 and look at the illustrations. Talk with a partner about what each side of the illustration shows.

Cite Text Evidence What clues tell you how the nests are alike and different? Use the chart to record your evidence.

Alike	Different

Write The author uses the illustrations to compare and contrast the nests of alligators to the nests of crocodiles _____

_____

QUICK TIP
When I reread, I can use illustrations and captions to help me understand complex ideas.

Your Turn

Does Gail Gibbons do a good job organizing the information so that you understand how alligators and crocodiles are alike and different? Use these sentence frames to organize your text evidence.

Gail Gibbons uses text features to...

The illustrations and captions tell me...

This helps me understand...

Go Digital!
Write your response online.

The Monkey and the Crocodile

1   Old Croc was the greatest hunter on the Congo River. All the wildlife that lived there feared him. The only animal he couldn't catch was Monkey. Each day he watched Monkey scamper fast, fast, across the rocks in the river to play with his friends.

2   One day, Old Croc came up with a plan. He would catch Monkey and have him for lunch. Old Croc hid in the river so his back stuck out of the water like a rock, and he waited for Monkey to cross. When Monkey stepped on his back, Old Croc grabbed his tail. "You're caught, Monkey! Now I will eat you," he growled.

Reread and use the prompts to take notes in the text.

Circle words in paragraph 1 that show what Old Croc is like. Underline the sentence that explains Old Croc's problem. Write his problem on the line.

_____

_____

COLLABORATE

Reread paragraph 2. Talk with a partner about Old Croc's plan. Make marks in the margin next to the steps that tell about how Old Croc planned to catch Monkey.

1. "Oh, but *you* can climb, Monkey," said Old Croc with a toothy grin. "Go pick a fruit and bring it back to me."

2. "No problem!" said Monkey, and with a *hop, hop* he jumped to the shore and climbed to the top of the tamarind tree. Then he laughed, "Old Croc, you have been tricked! You should know that a monkey is always too clever and fast to get caught by a crocodile."

3. With a grumble, Old Croc swam away and never tried to catch a monkey again.

Reread paragraph 1. Circle words and phrases that show how Old Croc is trying to trick Monkey.

COLLABORATE

Reread paragraphs 2 and 3. Talk with a partner about what the monkey does. Underline text evidence that supports your discussion.

What lesson does Old Croc learn? Draw a box around how you know and write it here:

_____

_____

_____

How does the author help you visualize what Old Croc and Monkey are like?

Talk About It Reread the excerpts on pages 190–191. Talk with a partner about what you picture about what each character is like.

Cite Text Evidence What words and phrases show what Old Croc and Monkey are like? Write text evidence in the chart.

Old Croc	Monkey

Write I can picture what the Old Croc and Monkey are like because the author _____

_____

_____

 **QUICK TIP**

I can use the author's words and phrases to help me visualize what the characters are like.

? How is what the photographer is doing in this photograph similar to the work of the author of *Alligators and Crocodiles*?

COLLABORATE

Talk About It Look at the photographer and read the caption. Talk with a partner about what the photographer in the photograph is doing.

Cite Text Evidence Underline how you know the photographer is being respectful of the penguins. Circle what he is using to do his job. Make notes in the margin next to the photograph telling how the penguins look.

Write The work of the photographer and the author are similar because

_____

_____

_____

_____

This photographer is studying a group of emperor penguins on Snow Hill Island, Antarctica.

Ollie's Escape

Literature Anthology:
pages 546–548

? How does the poet use words and phrases to make the poem funny?

COLLABORATE

Talk About It Reread page 547. Look at the illustration. Talk with a partner about what makes this poem funny.

Cite Text Evidence What words and phrases make the poem funny? Write text evidence in the chart.

Tip of the **Week**

When I **reread**, I can think about how the poet uses words and phrases. I look for text evidence to answer questions.

Text Evidence	How It Helps

Write The poet uses words and phrases to make the poem funny by

_____

_____

Jen

? **How does the poet use idioms to help you visualize the characters' actions?**

COLLABORATE

Talk About It Reread pages 547–548. Talk with a partner about what Principal Poole does when he sees Ollie.

Cite Text Evidence What words and phrases help you visualize the characters' actions? Write text evidence in the chart.

Idiom	What I Visualize

Write The author uses idioms to describe the characters' actions to

_____

_____

QUICK TIP

When I reread, I can see how the poet uses idioms to make the poem funny and to show the characters' actions.

Your Turn

How does the poet use words and phrases to help you understand how the characters in the poem feel about Ollie? Use these sentence frames to organize text evidence.

The poet uses sensory language to...

His words and phrases help me visualize...

This is important because it helps me understand...

Go Digital!
Write your response online.

The Gentleman Bookworm

? How does the illustration help you understand the details in the poem?

COLLABORATE

Talk About It Look at the illustration on pages 550 and 551. Talk with a partner about what the bookworms are doing.

Cite Text Evidence What clues in the illustration help you understand what the bookworms are doing? Write them in the chart.

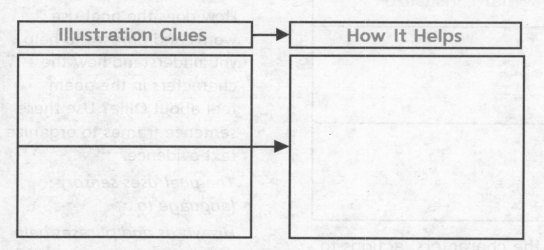

Illustration Clues →	How It Helps

Write The poet uses the illustration to _____

_____

How does the poet use personification to help you visualize what the bookworms are doing?

QUICK TIP
I can use poet's words to help me visualize what the characters in the poem are doing.

COLLABORATE

Talk About It With a partner, reread page 551. Talk about what the bookworms are doing that people usually do.

Cite Text Evidence What words and phrases describe things that people do? Write text evidence and tell how it helps you visualize.

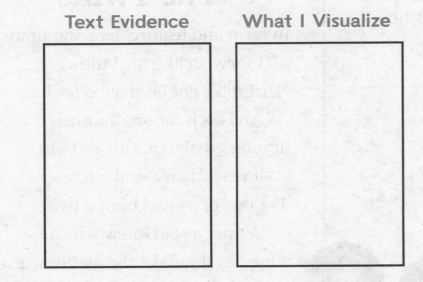

Text Evidence	What I Visualize

Write The poet uses personification in the poem by _____

_____

_____

_____

? How is the way poet Henry Leigh makes you feel similar to how the poets of "Ollie's Escape" and "The Gentleman's Bookworm" make you feel?

COLLABORATE

"Talk About It Read the excerpt from "The Twins." Talk with a partner about what is funny about the poem.

Cite Text Evidence Circle the words in the poem that rhyme. Underline what phrases are funny. Think about how the poet creates the tone or mood. Now think about how the other poems you read this week make you feel.

Write All three poets _____

_____

🔍 **QUICK TIP**

I see that the poet uses rhyming words and a bouncy rhythm. This will help me compare the poems.

From
"The Twins"

In form and feature, face and limb,
  I grew so like my brother,
That folks got taking me for him,
  And each for one another.
It puzzled all our kith and kin,
  It reach'd an awful pitch;
For one of us was born a twin,
  Yet not a soul knew which.
One day (to make the matter worse),
  Before our names were fix'd,
As we were being wash'd by nurse
  We got completely mix'd.

— Henry Leigh